ANTIQUITIES OF WEST MAYO

Antiquities of West Mayo

Christiaan Corlett

Wordwell

First published in 2001
Wordwell Ltd
PO Box 69, Bray, Co. Wicklow
Copyright © Wordwell 2001

ISBN 1 869857 48 8

British Library Cataloguing-in-Publication Data.
A catalogue record for this book is available from the British Library.

This publication has received support from the Heritage Council under the 2001 Publications Grant Scheme.

Copy-editor and indexer: Aisling Flood
Cover design: Rachel Dunne

Typeset in Ireland by Wordwell Ltd

Printed by Brookfield Printing Company

All photographs © Christiaan Corlett except where otherwise stated

Contents

List of plates

Acknowledgements

I would like to thank several people for providing me with much encouragement, information and hospitality over the years: Gerry and Ann Bracken from Westport; Noel O'Neill from Castlebar, Meike Blackwell from Rosbeg; Harry Hughes from Westport; David O'Dowd from Fallduff; Eoin Campbell from Murrisk; Jarlath Duffy, Aidan Clarke and Brona Joyce from Westport; Marion Irwin from Cashel; Sal O'Malley from Carrownisky; Christy Lawless from Turlough; and Ivor Hamrock from Mayo County Library.

I also thank my colleagues in the National Monuments and Architectural Protection Division, in particular Victor Buckley, David Sweetman, Con Manning, Tom Condit and Eamonn Cody. I am also indebted to my other archaeological colleagues, in particular Leo Morahan, Michael Gibbons, Gerry Walsh, Christina Fredengren, Christoph Oldenbourg, Karena Morton and Karl Brady. Furthermore, I wish to thank the staff of the National Museum of Ireland, in particular Mary Cahill, and the librarians of the Royal Society of Antiquaries of Ireland, the Royal Irish Academy and the National Library of Ireland for their valuable assistance.

Frontispiece—Standing stone at Derryheagh.

Introduction

This study focuses on the baronies of Burrishoole and Murrisk in West Mayo (see map on pp 102–3), stretching along the Atlantic coast from Killary Harbour in the south to Mulranny in the north and including the islands of Inishturk and Clare Island off the west coast. From Mulranny the boundary extends along the foothills of the Nephin Beg range of mountains, then in a line east of Newport, Westport and Aghagower, and from here along the Partry Mountains before reaching Killary Harbour. This area includes the parishes of Aghagower, Burrishoole, Kilgeever, Kilmeena, Kilmaclasser and Oughaval, and much of Islandeady parish. Included within the barony of Burrishoole is Achill Island, which has been the subject of separate research and is not included in this volume. Today it is the parish territorial division that is best known; however, in antiquity the baronial division was very important, and the baronies of Burrishoole and Murrisk once formed the ancient territory known as Umhall.

The landscape of this area is world-renowned for its powerful and sometimes terrific beauty. Travel writers of the nineteenth and twentieth centuries have been inspired by the diverse charms of this landscape and have rarely been stuck for words. This diversity is most frequently characterised by a common thread: a turbulent relationship between rock and water. However, a factor that has had an equally profound impact on the formation of the

Pl. 1— Askillaun stone rows.

PAST AND PRESENT
Everywhere, our past and present co-exist, but not always in harmony.

*Pl. 2—Westport
standing stone.*

STILL STANDING...

This Westport standing stone probably originally served to mark an ancestral territorial boundary; however, today it has been given a new function as a centrepiece in a residential estate. A careless mistake by a motorist could irreparably damage this site.

landscape as we know it today is human beings. This is not simply a recent impact that can be attributed to modern technology and culture but the result of several thousand years of human influence. Our past has shaped in so many ways our present, and we do not adequately acknowledge the achievements of those who came before us. The story of that human impact since the arrival of the first settlers is told here. It is a story with many gaps, from which stem many questions and suppositions. I trust that the telling of this story will not be seen as the final word. Instead, I hope it will create a hunger for answers to the many questions that remain—a hunger that can only be satisfied by future research. Furthermore, I hope that the telling of this story will awaken a realisation that our archaeological and historical background is our inheritance, and as such we are obliged to respect its importance and preserve it for future generations.

The work presented here is an attempt to condense an extensive wealth of archaeological and historical information and, through the selection of illustrations, to make the archaeology of West Mayo accessible to a wider audience. Many earlier scholars have made enormous contributions to the research of the archaeology of West Mayo, and this book is a dedication to those scholars.

The physical landscape

West Mayo is perhaps best known for the scenic beauty and drama of its mountains, valleys, lakes, coastline and islands. The underlying geological ingredients of this complex landscape were formed millions of years ago, long before the island of Ireland existed as we know it today. Among these geological ingredients are the quartzites of the Nephin Beg mountain range, which was formed during the Dalradian period, some 600–750 million years ago, unlike the quartzite peak of Croagh Patrick, which was formed during the Silurian period, some 410–440 million years ago. Towards the end of this period enormous mountain ranges were formed, and the resulting friction in the earth's crust created leakages of magma to the surface. This cooled slowly,

Pl. 3—Summit of Croagh Patrick.

'MADE TO CHEER AND TO DELIGHT'

Inspired by the natural beauties of West Mayo, several nineteenth-century travel writers tried to outdo one another in their descriptions of the landscape. T.O. Russell in his *Beauties and antiquities of Ireland* (1897) wrote that Croagh Patrick 'seems to have been made to cheer and to delight, and not to terrify or to startle. It seems to have said to the mountains round it—"Stand back; come not too near me lest your shadows fall on me and hide, even for an instant, one gleam of my radiant loveliness." So the mountains round it do stand back, and this is the one cause of its winsomeness, rightness, and cheerfulness'.

forming the coarse-grained granite that can be found around Louisburgh. The enormous mountain ranges of the Silurian period were gradually eroded over several million years during the Devonian period, 360–410 million years ago. The landscape at that time was a desert, and the occasional flash floods caused by torrential rain eroded the mountains over time and deposited the sands in sheets on the plains, forming the Old Red Sandstones that can be found today along the northern shores of Clew Bay. Beneath the rolling plains between Newport and Westport are limestones formed during the Carboniferous period over 300 million years ago, when the landscape changed to one of tropical seas. These stones today contain the fossils of the marine life that once inhabited those waters. Limestone is very soluble, and water has frequently penetrated deep into this bedrock. So much so that entire rivers, such as the Aille River near Aghagower, disappear into caverns deep below the surface. Heavy rainfall can cause the level of the river to rise suddenly in the Aille caverns, and the flood waters have become known as the *Tuille Sidhe,* 'the fairy tide'.

Pl. 4—Clew Bay and Croagh Patrick.

CLEW BAY

William Thackeray, who visited the area in 1842, in his *Irish sketch-book* (1843) described what he saw: 'the bay, with the Reek, which sweeps down to the sea, and a hundred islands in it, were dressed up in gold and purple, and crimson, with the whole cloudy west in a flame'.

MWEELREA AND THE SHEEFFRY HILLS

Mweelrea and the Sheeffry Hills consist of grits, sandstones, slates and shales that underwent volcanic activity during the Ordovician period, between 440 and 510 million years ago. Originally these mountains formed a large, table-like plateau, but they were broken up by faulting and fracturing caused by movement of the earth's crust. Doo Lough Valley was formed by such fracturing and during the Ice Age became enhanced and deepened by ice that followed the course of the existing valley.

Pl. 5—The Sheeffry Hills and Mweelrea.

Pl. 6—Doo Lough Valley.

Pl. 7—Mweelrea and Killary Harbour.

KILLARY HARBOUR

High on the southern slopes of Mweelrea are a number of corries, the steep-sided nests where glaciers were born and nurtured before growing in strength and leaving to explore the world below. The glacier that formed in this corry is one of a number that combined to carve out the long, narrow valley that, after the ice melted, was drowned by the Atlantic waters to form Killary Harbour.

Pl. 8—Clare Island.

CLARE ISLAND

At the mouth of Clew Bay is Clare Island, dominated by the mountain of Knockmore, from which the Atlantic has carved some of the highest cliffs in Ireland. A multidisciplinary survey was carried out on the island between 1909 and 1911, under the direction of Robert Lloyd Praeger, and published by the Royal Irish Academy. It studied the geology, placenames, archaeology, and animal and plant life. The archaeological survey was undertaken by Thomas J. Westropp and George Fogarty. This was the first large-scale and comprehensive survey of its kind carried out in Ireland.

Water has enhanced the visual delights of these geological ingredients in various ways, in particular in its most voracious form, ice, which developed after the cooling of the climate some two million years ago. The Ice Age spawned glaciers in the mountains, later forming corry lakes with their steep-sided cliffs, such as Lough Glenawough in the Partry Mountains overlooking the Erriff Valley, and also along the north-facing slopes of the Sheeffry Hills. These great sheets of ice crept slowly out from the slopes of Mweelrea, the Sheeffry Hills and the Nephin Beg mountain range north of Clew Bay. The ice also sculpted several steep-sided valleys, such as the Glenummera Valley, where a weakness in the rock was exploited and the less resistant band of slate was more easily carved by the ice than the surrounding rocks. As the glaciers advanced through the valleys, they gouged out hollows that later filled with water to form lakes,

Pl. 9—Ancient forest drowned in Lough Nahaltora.

LOUGH NAHALTORA

Much of the West Mayo landscape became dominated by blanket bog around 4000 years ago. For a time the climate appears to have warmed and forests of pine flourished in the bog. However, the climate became wetter again, replenishing the bog, which became too wet for the trees. The stumps of these trees have frequently been preserved by the bog that killed them, and at Lough Nahaltora the lake waters have eroded the peat, thereby exposing their mummified corpses.

such as those in Doo Lough Valley. The sheets of ice descended from the mountains and met on the lower ground between Westport and Newport. The movement of the ice in this area carved out hollows and dumped the offcuts as hills. These were rounded off by the ice-sheets, and when the ice finally disappeared these dumps remained in the form of distinctive rounded hills known as drumlins. Much of this landscape became flooded by the sea, creating Clew Bay, where the drumlin hills protrude above the waters as islands.

The ice-sheets finally retreated northwards around 10,000 years ago, allowing plant and animal life to expand across the island. Hazel and pine woodlands gradually developed, and over time deciduous hardwood trees came to dominate the countryside, in particular oak, elm and ash. Among the first wildlife to colonise Ireland were humans, around 9000 years ago, at which time much of the island was covered in dense hazel and oak forests. This forestry disappeared from mountain areas and the poorer soils along the west coast and was gradually replaced by blanket bog, which typically covers these slopes today. This blanket bog began to develop around 4000 years ago, largely owing to climatic deterioration and human interference. For example, early farmers who cleared woodlands removed an important consumer of rainwater that was then trapped in the soil. This process may have been aided by an increase in rainfall, and the waterlogged soils encouraged the widespread growth of sphagnum moss, the primary ingredient of blanket bog. In these waterlogged conditions sphagnum moss does not decompose in the normal way and instead accumulates to form bog. After several thousand years this bog can build up to several metres above the original ground level.

The Stone Age

THE EARLIEST HUMAN SETTLERS

At a time when Ireland was largely covered by enormous sheets of ice, humans had settled throughout much of Europe. It seems that the ice-sheets may have deterred the human instinct to explore as far west in Europe as Ireland, even though there were frequently periods when much of the island was devoid of ice. The earliest known settlers arrived not long after the retreat of the ice-sheets, around 9000 years ago. This period is known to archaeologists as the Mesolithic, or Middle Stone Age. As the term suggests, stone dominated the technology of this period, although other raw materials such as wood and bone were also used.

At this time Ireland was heavily wooded, with tall canopy forestry dominating the fertile plains and hazel scrub on rougher ground. Many of the lakes of the Irish midlands became choked with vegetation, with the result that bogs began to develop. The coastline was constantly changing with rising and falling sea levels. This landscape supported diverse wildlife, including pig, red deer and a variety of birds. Lakes, rivers and, in particular, the coast supported a wide selection of fish. This was very important to the earliest settlers, who depended on hunting, fishing and gathering food such as fruit and nuts in the forests. This type of economy could probably only support small, mobile groups, perhaps consisting of an extended family. The temporary houses of these nomadic hunters and fishers have long since disappeared, and they left no religious monuments. Their temples may have been the mountains and rivers that surrounded them. One of the few traces of evidence for these people are the distinctive stone tools they left behind. Only one such artefact has been found in West Mayo, a tool called a Bann Flake from Burrishoole. Perhaps one day the elusive archaeological evidence for these wandering hunters and fishers will come to light in West Mayo, but at present the best evidence for early human settlers in this area dates to the New Stone Age, or Neolithic, when people were dependent on a very different type of economy—farming.

THE BEGINNINGS OF AGRICULTURE

In around 4000 BC, farming was introduced to Ireland, following its initial development in the Middle East some 5000 years before. The arrival of farming in Ireland brought many changes and required a different way of thinking and a new way of life from the hunting and gathering of before. One of the first requirements was to introduce the very materials of farming, i.e. cereals, cattle and sheep, all of which were not native to Ireland. Also, the land had to be cleared of trees in order to make the fields suitable for keeping stock or planting crops. The trees could be felled using fire or stone axes, such as a fine

TOOLS AND WEAPONS

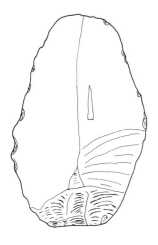

Fig. 1—Burrishoole Bann Flake.

This flint object, 6.5cm long, from Burrishoole is an example of a Bann Flake, so called because they were first recognised in large numbers by archaeologists along the River Bann. They are typically trimmed or shaped at the butt end and were worked along the edges in order to sharpen them. Bann Flakes may have been used for hunting or fishing or as knives in food preparation and other domestic chores. Many would originally have been hafted in a wooden handle. This Mesolithic tool from Burrishoole was reused in modern times as a charm.

Fig. 2—Stone axes from Rockfleet and Burrishoole.

Experiments have demonstrated that stone axes could be used successfully for felling trees. One of the two axes from Rockfleet (far right) appears more like an adze and may have been used for more sophisticated carpentry. However, it is clear that some axes also served as status symbols, and recent research indicates that they may have played an important role in ceremonies. In modern times the stone axe from Burrishoole was believed to cure cattle.

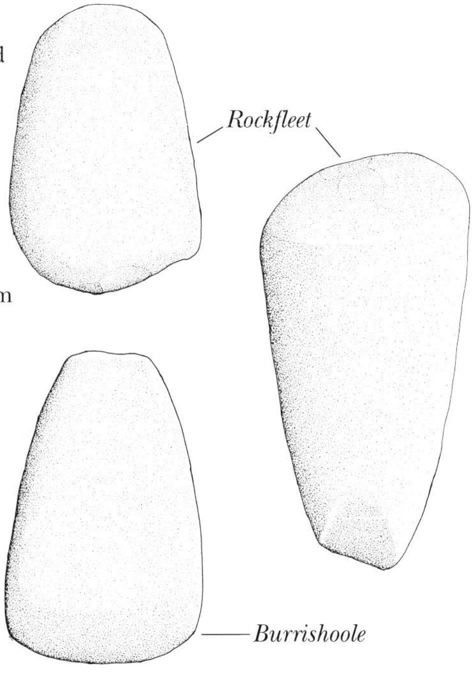

Rockfleet

Burrishoole

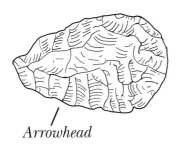

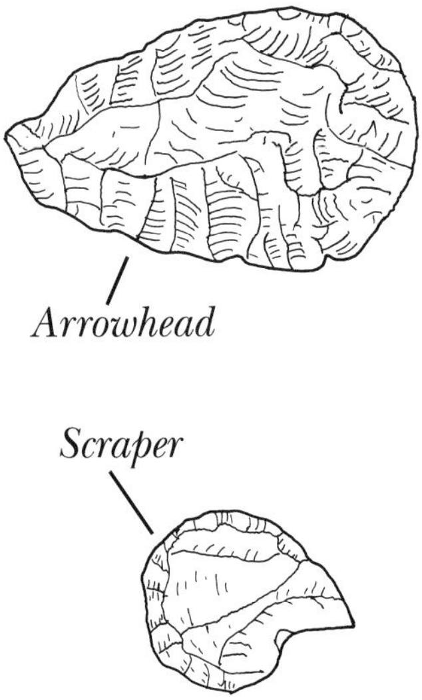

Arrowhead

Scraper

Fig. 3—Letterkeen chert arrowhead and flint scraper.

The Letterkeen leaf-shaped arrowhead, 4.5cm long, is typical of Stone Age arrowheads and is made of a blackish stone called chert. The flint thumb scraper could be used for a variety of purposes such as cleaning animal hides or fine woodworking.

Pl. 10—Axe found at Rockfield near Kilbree (courtesy of the National Museum of Ireland ©).

A flint axehead, partly polished, was found in 1971 during turf-cutting in a bog called Tourlafeen at Rockfield near Kilbree. A bog is an unusual place to find a stone axe. Could this have been lost in the bog by its owner, or was it deliberately cast away as some form of religious offering?

flint example from Rockfield near Aghagower. Extensive areas of highly organised field systems dating to around 5000 years ago have been found at the Céide Fields in north Mayo. These consist of stone walls that had become covered by blanket bog over 4000 years ago and were uncovered by turf-cutting in modern times. On more fertile soils, not affected by blanket bog, these early field systems were not preserved and were altered by farmers over the millennia. Stone walls similar to those at the Céide Fields have been found beneath the mountain bogs on Clare Island and may have been made by the earliest farmers on the island over 5000 years ago. Such walls have also been found on the mainland, for example at Formoyle near a megalithic tomb that dates to this period.

Farming required a greater degree of permanency, and families and communities needed long-term dwellings. A number of these early houses have been found in Ireland, including an example at Ballyglass in north Mayo. Typically they were large, rectangular houses built of timber. This early farming period is termed the Neolithic, or New Stone Age, after changes in the stone technology used. This technology consisted of a range of stone objects such as knives, scrapers, arrowheads and axeheads. A chert arrowhead and a flint scraper from Letterkeen in the north of the region are typical of stone tools from this period. However, apart from a number of axeheads, few objects of this period have been found in West Mayo. Unlike the previous, Mesolithic period,

THE DEPTHS OF TIME

Peeping through the bog on the slopes of Knockmore, at the edge of the cliffs of Clare Island, are the collapsed stone field walls built by some of the earliest farmers in this region. Over time the fields these farmers once toiled became engulfed by the bog and they remained hidden for thousands of years. It is only in more recent times when turf became an important fuel that we have delved almost literally into the depths of time, towards the old ground on which our ancestors walked and farmed.

Pl. 11—Pre-bog wall on Clare Island.

the Neolithic is characterised by large-scale religious structures conceived as permanent monuments in the landscape. The best-known of these are megalithic tombs.

MEGALITHIC TOMBS

Many early farming communities in Ireland constructed megalithic tombs as monuments to their dead. The term 'megalithic' derives from the Greek words for big stones. Evidence from a number of excavated megalithic tombs suggests that only the community leaders were buried within them. Even so, it would require the efforts of an entire community to engineer and construct these

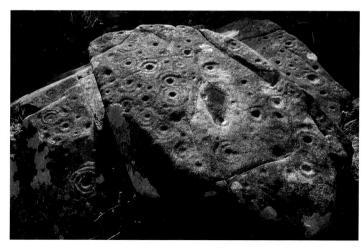

Pl. 12—*Rock art at Boheh.*

Pl. 13—*Sun rolling down the side of Croagh Patrick on 24 April 1992 (photo courtesy of Gerry Bracken ©).*

ROCK ART

The cup- and ringmarks that cover the large natural outcrop of rock at Boheh belong to a style of art dating to the end of the Stone Age. The stone was later Christianised in name and is still called St Patrick's Chair. In 1989 Gerry Bracken from Westport noted that from this stone on 18 April and 24 August the sun appears to roll down the side of Croagh Patrick as it sets. This stone is the only fixed place in the landscape from which this rolling sun spectacle can be seen, and this seems to be the reason that it was chosen by the artists. The dates may have been used to celebrate the sowing and harvest seasons.

LEABA DHIARMAID AGUS GRÁINNE

According to legend, a marriage was arranged between Gráinne, daughter of the high king of Ireland, and the aging Fionn Mac Cumhail, legendary leader of the mythical band of warriors called the Fianna. However, at the wedding feast at Tara, Co. Meath, Gráinne was overcome with love for one of Fionn's company, Diarmuid (reputedly the best lover of women in the whole world). During the feast she cast a sleeping spell on all the company except Diarmuid. While Fionn Mac Cumhail slept, Gráinne put a druid's spell on Diarmuid and forced him to take her from Tara. They travelled throughout the country with Fionn in pursuit, and every night Diarmuid built a house for himself and Gráinne to take shelter in. The megalithic tombs at Aillemore and Formoyle were called *Leaba Dhiarmaid agus Gráinne*, 'the bed of Diarmuid and Gráinne', in modern folk tradition.

In fact, these court tombs were built over 5000 years ago, during the Stone Age, and mark the burial places of the earliest Irish farmers. The tomb at Formoyle is only a skeleton of the original; however, this tomb at Aillemore preserves important evidence of the roofing of these tombs.

Pl. 14—Aillemore court tomb.

monuments. The most common form of megalithic tomb in West Mayo is the court tomb, so called because of the arrangement of stones forming an open-air court in front of the entrance to the tomb. This court appears to reflect the communal nature of the funerary rituals and ceremonies that took place during this period. Indeed, many of these tombs may also have been used as monuments for other religious ceremonies during the year.

Unfortunately, of the five court tombs known in West Mayo, none has a well-preserved court. Typically the burial gallery of these tombs was divided into two chambers, separated by an arrangement of stones forming a sill and jambs. This is best preserved in the court tomb on Clare Island and, in particular, at Aillemore near Killadoon. The Aillemore tomb also has very good evidence of the roofing of the burial gallery, which took the form of steeply pitched drystone corbelling of large slabs. All but the final capstones of this roof survive intact at Aillemore.

The Early Bronze Age

THE BEGINNINGS OF METALWORKING

In around 2500 BC the concept of metalworking was brought to Ireland, and metal very gradually began to replace stone as the dominant raw material. Ireland had large resources of several metals, in particular copper and gold. Indeed, these were the most commonly used metals in Europe at this time, and it has been suggested that Ireland was a source of some of the copper and gold used elsewhere in north-west Europe. West Mayo has only small resources of copper; however, there are large amounts of gold known in the Croagh Patrick area, in particular in the Owenwee River, hence its name in Irish, *Abhainn buí*, 'yellow river'.

Copper was most commonly used to produce axes and daggers. Later, tin was mixed with copper to form bronze, which produced a stronger cutting edge than copper. Bronze was used to make more sophisticated objects such as palstaves—a form of axehead. One such palstave was found at Newport. Gold was used to produce adornments such as lunulae, typically Irish neck ornaments. At this time gold was worked by hammering, and any decoration was lightly incised onto the surface of the object.

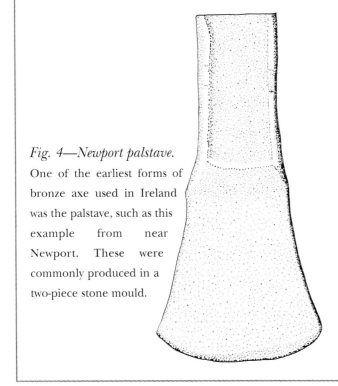

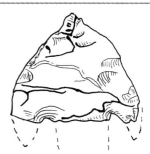

Fig. 4—Newport palstave.
One of the earliest forms of bronze axe used in Ireland was the palstave, such as this example from near Newport. These were commonly produced in a two-piece stone mould.

Fig. 5—Capnagower barbed and tanged arrowhead (after Gosling 1993).
Despite the invention of metal production, stone continued to be used to make many utensils, in particular tiny barbed and tanged arrowheads such as this chert example, only 1.5cm wide, found in a shell midden at the northern end of the beach near the harbour on Clare Island. These are highly accomplished pieces, and their entire surface has been carefully shaped and worked.

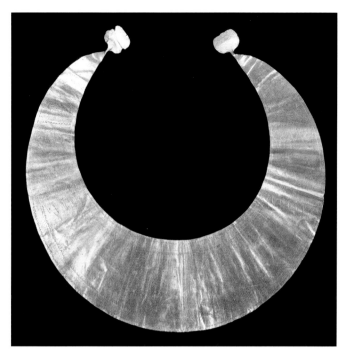

Pl. 15—Lunula from West Mayo (courtesy of the National Museum of Ireland ©).

JEWELLERY

Alongside the production of copper and bronze artefacts was the earliest manufacture of gold objects in Ireland, such as this gold lunula, or neck ornament (weighing 46.33g), which was found in the nineteenth century during turf-cutting at an unrecorded location on the west coast of Mayo. Apparently a second was found at the same time, but it was sold to a jeweller.

In around 1901 a collection of 78 stone beads from a necklace was found over 4ft deep in a bog somewhere near Westport. The steatite beads are disc-like and grey. They average about 1.5cm across and only 4mm thick. Their style seems to compare with beads found elsewhere in Ireland that have been dated to the Neolithic and Early Bronze Age.

Pl. 16—Beads from a bog near Westport (courtesy of the National Museum of Ireland ©).

BURIAL TRADITIONS

From 2500 to 1500 BC, burial rites became tremendously varied. At the beginning of the period megalithic tombs known as wedge tombs were commonly used. A near-perfectly preserved wedge tomb survives at Srahwee near Killadoon. These tombs are named after their characteristic wedge shape, clearly seen at Srahwee. In general, however, less complicated burial monuments were used, such as stone cairns on upland areas. One such cairn is perched on the eastern shoulder of Croagh Patrick, overlooking Lough Nacorra. On more low-lying ground, earthen mounds were more often used to

Pl. 17—Srahwee wedge tomb.

SRAHWEE WEDGE TOMB

This small wedge tomb is one of the best-preserved examples in the country. They are so called because of their wedge shape, wider and higher at the entrance and gradually tapering towards the rear. This form of tomb is generally dated to the beginning of the Bronze Age and belonged to a final flourish of megalithic tomb construction in Ireland.

Pl. 18—Teevenacroaghy cairn.

MYTHICAL MONSTERS

This small cairn, on the eastern shoulder of Croagh Patrick overlooking Lough Nacorra, probably covers an Early Bronze Age burial. There are reasons to believe that Croagh Patrick was a sacred mountain at this time and that Lough Nacorra was a sacred lake, perhaps the dwelling of a pagan water god. Legend tells that when St Patrick visited the mountain he was tormented by Caorthannach, the devil's mother assuming the shape of a serpent. Patrick banished this demon into the lake below, which was named Lough Nacorra after the serpent. According to another legend, recorded by John O'Donovan of the Ordnance Survey, before 'Patrick's conflict with the demons there was no lake there, but he drove Corra, the fiercest of them, into this hollow with so much violence that he caused the lake to spring forth'. Caesar Otway during his 1838 tour of Connacht was told by a local guide that 'there the serpent is fastened alive to the bottom, but in the time of storm, when thunder is rolling, and lightning flashing and frightening away the dark night, then the serpent is allowed to rise and take its sport on the surface; and when by any chance man at this time pass that lonely water they see the serpent riding the waves like a wild horse with a flowing mane; the froth boiling away from his sides, and all is terrible entirely.' These legends of a terrible serpent or monster in Lough Nacorra may represent a Christian denunciation of a pagan deity who was believed to inhabit the lake.

DEVLIN SOUTH CAIRN

On the highest peak of the hills of Devlin and Killadoon is a cairn, probably marking an Early Bronze Age burial. The original cairn can be seen beneath a modern cairn that was probably built by the Ordnance Survey during the nineteenth century using the stones of the older cairn. From here are some of the most dramatic views along the Atlantic coast.

Pl. 19—Devlin South cairn.

cover burials. The best-preserved example of such a burial mound is at Sheean overlooking Croagh Patrick, Clew Bay and Westport. The types of burial that these cairns and mounds probably cover may be similar to the cemetery found during the excavations at Letterkeen. This consisted of a number of stone-lined graves containing cremations that were accompanied by pottery vessels.

Pl. 20—Selection of Early Bronze Age pottery from Letterkeen (courtesy of the National Museum of Ireland ©).

POTTERY

Excavations at Letterkeen found that during the early medieval period a ringfort had been built on top of an Early Bronze Age cemetery, which may have been covered originally by a mound or cairn. Five stone-lined graves were found containing the cremated human remains of about twelve individuals, representing adults and children. Accompanying several of the burials were these pots, called food vessels because it is generally believed that they contained food offerings for the journey of the deceased into the afterlife. There was also a tiny pot, called a pygmy cup, a type that is believed by some to have contained incense.

This vase-shaped food vessel was found in 1954 in a cist at Cashel covered by a mound of earth and stones. The cist consisted of two compartments: one was empty but the other contained the remains of a pot, which is shown here reconstructed. It seems that the grave had been opened some fifty years before by a local clergyman who uncovered the 'crock' and returned the pieces to the grave.

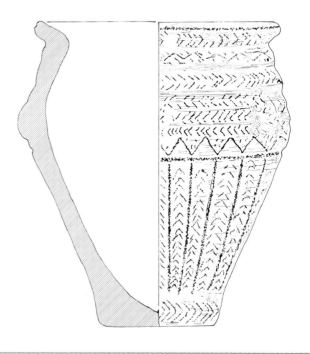

Fig. 6—Cashel food vessel (after Rynne 1954–6).

The Late Bronze Age and Iron Age: the end of prehistory

Pl. 21—
Formoyle
standing
stone.

The period from 1200 to 600 BC is known as the Late Bronze Age but has also been called the Golden Age of prehistoric Ireland. During this time bronze was still used to make weapons and tools. The socketed form of bronze axe was developed during this period, and a number of examples are known from West Mayo, for example from Kilbride and Newport. Bronze was sometimes used for personal adornments, such as two sunflower pins from Newport. However, the period is best known for the quality and quantity of gold objects. Several beautiful gold pieces are known from West Mayo, including a bracelet and dress-fastener from Kilbride. Such an emphasis on gold suggests that certain elements of society had accumulated great wealth, which usually brings new concerns for weaponry and defence, reflected by a bronze sword from Westport and a spearhead from Newport.

FULACHTA FIADH

Evidence for more mundane, domestic activity during the Bronze Age can be

Fig. 7—Socketed axes from Derryloughan East, Lecarrow and Tonlegee.

Several socketed bronze axes are known from West Mayo. The socket was invented to allow more effective hafting of these axes. The axe from Lecarrow was found at the south end of the townland in a drain at the bottom of a hill called *Cnocán na gCeann*, 'the hill of the heads'. According to local folklore, a chieftain named Leachtain was killed in a battle here, and his grave is marked by a whitethorn bush.

Fig. 8—Westport sword (right) and Newport spearhead (far right) (after Eogan 1965; 1983).

Swords and spearheads are good evidence of the rise in warfare during this period. This fine 60cm-long bronze sword, dated to 1000–700 BC, was found in a bog near Westport in 1854. The blade is 4.3cm wide and only 7mm thick. The Newport spearhead is over 12cm long and was part of a hoard of bronze objects including several axes and decorative pins.

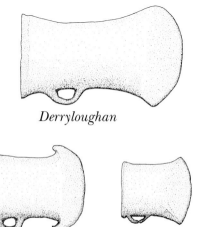

Derryloughan

Lecarrow   Tonlegee

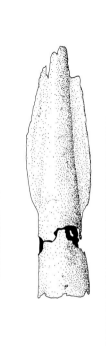

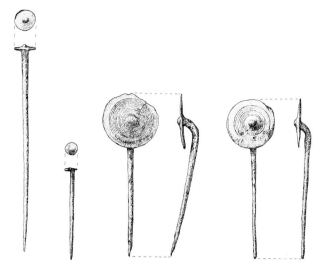

Fig. 9—Newport hoard (after Eogan 1983). This selection of artefacts from a hoard of objects found near Newport includes a bronze spearhead and two socketed axes (not illustrated), as well as these two disc-headed pins and two sunflower pins used as jewellery to fasten clothing.

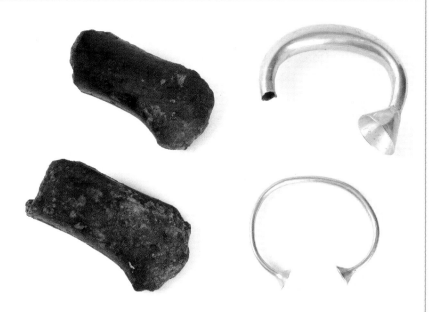

Pl. 22—Gold and bronze hoard from Kilbride (courtesy of the National Museum of Ireland ©).

GOLD

Towards the end of the Bronze Age, around 700 BC, Irish goldworking became highly developed and accomplished, producing some of the most spectacular gold artefacts from any period in Irish history or prehistory. A gold bracelet (weighing just over 20g) and a gold dress-fastener (both above) were found together with two bronze axes under the corner of a boulder standing in a field at Kilbride. The bracelet is undecorated, but the marks of the hammer used in its production are clearly seen. The dress-fastener originally had two terminals, but only one survives, shaped like a trumpet. It is also decorated with lightly incised triangles forming a chevron-type design and bands of diagonal lines forming a herringbone pattern.

A gold bracelet in two parts was found by a farmer sowing potatoes in a field in Carrowbeg, Kilmeena.

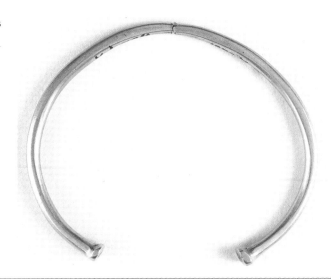

Pl. 23—Gold bracelet from Kilmeena (courtesy of the National Museum of Ireland ©).

Pl. 24— Devlin North fulacht fiadh.

Pl. 25— Wooden trough from Raigh near Aghagower (courtesy of Christy Lawless ©).

FULACHTA FIADH

Typically *fulachta fiadh* are situated beside a stream to provide clean water to fill a stone or timber trough. Stones were heated on a nearby fire and then used to heat the water in the trough. The heated water could be maintained at boiling point with the addition every so often of hot stones from the fire. Over time the discarded burnt stones accumulated in a horseshoe shape around the trough.

found in the form of *fulachta fiadh*. In some areas of the country, folklore associates these sites with the hunting parties of the Fianna, the burnt stone being left over from cooking their kill. According to the folk traditions of Burrishoole, they were used by the Danes for making beer from heather. Typically a *fulacht fiadh* consists of a horseshoe-shaped mound of burnt stone. Excavations of a number of these sites have uncovered wooden troughs immediately beside the mounds. These troughs were filled with water, and heated stones were placed within in order to boil the water. One such trough was found accidentally when an agricultural drain was dug beside a *fulacht fiadh* at Raigh near Aghagower. Archaeological excavations have shown that these sites were most commonly used between 1500 and 1000 BC, although the wooden trough from Raigh dates to around 900 BC. Although they are most commonly associated with cooking, little evidence for this has been found during archaeological excavations of these sites. Perhaps, then, the hot water produced at *fulachta fiadh* had a range of other uses, such as in textile manufacture.

Fulachta fiadh are one of the most numerous prehistoric sites in the country, and also in West Mayo, with 150 known on Clare Island alone. At Devlin near Killadoon are two well-preserved *fulachta fiadh* back to back. Nearby is a stone enclosure, which may be a contemporary settlement site. Leo Morahan has recently identified a group of three *fulachta fiadh* at Glaspatrick and four more at Bellataleen on the northern slopes of Croagh Patrick.

STANDING STONES

During this period various standing stone monuments became popular places of ceremony and worship. Standing stones had been used since the Neolithic, but it appears that they became most popular during the Bronze Age and Iron Age. In more recent times, several standing stones near Newport were known as *fir bréige*, 'scarecrows'. Standing stones are often dramatic monuments in the landscape, and it is difficult not to be impressed by the scale of some examples, such as the enormous stone at Cross strand. Some stand alone, whereas at Killadangan they form part of a large complex, consisting of scattered standing stones and a row of four stones. This row is aligned with the setting sun of the winter solstice, and its function was clearly to celebrate the shortest day of the year. This was the prehistoric New Year's Eve. However, the stone rows at Askillaun are not aligned with the setting or rising sun, and the function of this site is much more difficult to explain. Similarly, many of the single standing stones scattered throughout the West Mayo countryside are difficult to interpret. They may have been used for a variety of religious or political purposes, for example as burial markers or political boundary markers. Others appear to have marked routeways.

Ring-barrows, such as at Liscarney, consist of a simple circular earthen mound enclosed by a ditch and an outer bank. Excavations of these sites elsewhere in Ireland show that the cremated remains of individuals were placed

Pl. 26—Liscarney standing stone.

Pl. 27—Standing stone at Rusheen near Carraholly.

STANDING STONES

The function of standing stones remains a mystery, although there can be no doubt that their apparent simplicity masks a whole range of rituals and ceremonies carried out at these sites. Some examples elsewhere in the country have been found to mark burials. Others probably do not mark burials, and another explanation must be put forward. Perhaps they were territorial markers, or possibly they recorded important places in the landscape where an event took place. From the standing stones at Liscarney and Rusheen there is a panoramic view of Croagh Patrick, which seems to have become a sacred mountain long before the arrival of St Patrick.

Pl. 28a and b—Standing stone called 'Clogh Patrick' at Lanmore.

CLOGH PATRICK

Some standing stones are located on the *Tóchar Phádraig*, the Christian pilgrim road to Croagh Patrick. Perhaps these stones mark the route of an earlier, pagan pilgrim road to the Reek. From the Lanmore stone, known as 'Clogh Patrick' ('Patrick's stone'), only the summit of the mountain can be seen, providing a teasing glimpse to pilgrims of their final goal. This needle-like stone was also known as *Clogh fhada*, 'the tall stone'.

near the centre of the mound and were sometimes accompanied by grave-goods or pottery. Ring-barrows have been variously dated to the Bronze Age and the Iron Age and were clearly a burial monument that stayed in use for a considerable time in Ireland. Typically these burial sites are small compared to Neolithic megalithic tombs or the large Early Bronze Age burial mounds such as at Sheean. However, their apparent insignificance in scale compared to these earlier monuments tends to mask the fact that these small ring-barrows were the burial places of the rich and powerful rulers of late prehistoric society.

THE IRON AGE

In around 600 BC new influences came to Ireland that gradually introduced the knowledge and use of iron, although for several centuries bronze continued to be used widely. This period is known as the Iron Age and continued in Ireland until the arrival of Christianity in around AD 400. This is the period that has frequently been associated with the coming of the Celts to Ireland, and elsewhere in Europe great civilisations, such as the Roman Empire, rose and fell. However, the Iron Age in Ireland is problematic for archaeologists. For example, very few artefacts dating to this period have been found in West Mayo, and without excavation it cannot be determined whether several of the monuments in the region, such as ring-barrows or standing stones, date to the Late Bronze Age or the Iron Age. The epic stories of warriors, kings and queens are traditionally believed to be of Celtic origin; however, they are best described as old Irish folk tales that have little connection with the so-called Celtic tribes of Europe that are supposed to have arrived in Ireland sometime before the birth of Christ. These stories, first recorded in writing by early medieval Irish monks, recall many heroic deeds, and the most famous of these are told in the conflicts between Medb, queen of Connacht, and Conor MacNessa, king of Ulster. In one early medieval poem, warriors of Connacht such as Corrgenn and Fraech (after whom Carnfree near Rathcroghan in County Roscommon is called) have strong associations with West Mayo. In an early eleventh-century poem written by MacLiag, bard of Brian Boru, after a legendary battle in which the champion Conall of the mythical Fir Bolg was killed his companions Ceat, Ross and Cuchullain were also killed and buried:

> In the tombs of Finnmaighe ['fair plain']
> Hence the Mound of the Heads is so called
> Above the strongly fortified Rath Umaill.

These poems and legends were written long after the end of the Iron Age, and they are based on fantasy rather than fact. However, they may shed some light on the Iron Age and preserve some early names in the area. For example, the Mound of the Heads may be the area known as *Cnocán na gCeann*, 'the hill of the heads', at Raigh near Burrishoole. However, it seems likely that the poems and legends that tell of mythical tribes inhabiting Ireland before the arrival of Christianity reflect more the times in which they were written than a glorious past.

This leaves us with the problem that in West Mayo, as in much of Ireland, there is no clear evidence for a Celtic presence. Indeed, until the arrival of Christianity the archaeological evidence provides very few clues about people's lives during those centuries from 600 BC to AD 400, a period in which surely many stories await to be told. However, history is not totally silent about the end

Pls 29a and b—Killadangan stone row.

Pl. 30—Killadangan stone row from north-north-east.

Pl. 31— Killadangan stone row at sunset on 21 December 1994.

THE LAZY SERVANT

Among the standing stones at Killadangan is a row of four stones that increase in height from north to south. As one looks south down the line of the stones, the eye is drawn up to a niche in the shoulder of Croagh Patrick, which forms the horizon. At 1.45p.m. on 21 December, the shortest day of the year, the sun sets within this niche, and at this point the sun is directly in line with the row of stones. Shortly afterwards the sun disappears behind the mountain.

A folk tale associated with these stones was recalled at the turn of the nineteenth century by a local storyteller, James Berry, in which the king of Killadangan is the brother of the first husband of Queen Maeve, the powerful Celtic queen of the west of Ireland. The name of this 'great pagan king' seems to have disappeared from local tradition, whereas the name of his lazy servant, Thulera, remains in folk memory. In this story the king made a vain attempt to force the sea and tide under his command. As the king awaited the incoming tide, his servant fell asleep, and the monarch was forced to fight a single-handed battle, wielding his sword against the encroaching sea. Both the king and his lazy servant drowned for their efforts.

*Pl. 32a
and b—
Stone pair
at Cross.*

AN STOCA MÓR AGUS AN STOCA BEAG

In a field beside the strand at Cross near Killadoon are two standing stones known locally as *an stoca mór agus an stoca beag*, 'the big stone and the little stone', and tradition holds that they were thrown there by a giant from Clare Island.

THE STONES OF THE FIANNA

Standing stones at Askillaun near Louisburgh, overlooking Clare Island, are known as *na clocha Fianna*, 'the stones of the Fianna'. The Fianna were the legendary warriors led by the mythic Celtic hero Fionn Mac Cumhail.

of the Iron Age, when Christianity began to make inroads into Irish society in the fifth century AD. One of the earliest Christian missionaries to Ireland was St Patrick, who allegedly came to Croagh Patrick to spend forty days and nights in penance. That he came here at all is significant, and according to legend his purpose in coming to Croagh Patrick was to confront a pagan king or deity there known as Crom Dubh. At the beginning of the nineteenth century the mountain was most commonly climbed by local pilgrims on *Aoine Crom Dubh*, the last Friday in July, coinciding with the ancient Celtic festival of Lughnasa. Clearly Croagh Patrick was a sacred mountain at the time of Patrick and probably had been for hundreds if not thousands of years.

Pl. 33—Askillaun stone row.

Pl. 34—Lugmore, Doo Lough Valley.

KING OF THE FAIRIES

In folklore, mountains such as Mweelrea and the Sheeffry Hills were often treated with superstition. The name Sheeffry may derive from the Irish word *sidh*, 'fairy'. According to one folk tradition, Lugmore, the valley in Mweelrea overlooking the north end of Doo Lough Valley, was one of the places where Finbarra, king of the Connacht fairies, held his court. Such superstitions may originate from a period before the arrival of Christianity when people appear to have believed that many places in the landscape around them were inhabited by supernatural beings.

BEEHIVE QUERN

This is an example of a beehive quern from Boheh, named after its domed shape like a beehive. This was the first form of rotary quern used in Ireland, during the centuries around the birth of Christ. The grain was fed into the funnel-shaped hopper at the top of the quern, and

Fig. 10— Boheh beehive quern.

from here it passed through the pipe onto the grinding surface. In the side of the quern is a hole for a wooden handle, which in turn may have been attached to a leather strap. A degree of strength was required to turn the quern, which is quite heavy. The quern measures 39cm across and 18.5cm high.

The early Middle Ages

THE DAWN OF HISTORY

Pl. 35—Kilgeever cross pillar.

With the arrival of Christianity in around AD 400 came the earliest historical writings in Ireland. However, there were only a few centres of writing during the early centuries of Christianity in Ireland, and detailed documentation of people, places and events only became widespread well over 1000 years later. As a result, there is a bias in the early writings towards the most important churches in Ireland and their clergy. West Mayo was not among the areas that received detailed documentation by the earliest writers, and we have only fragmentary accounts of its people and places during this time. We know from the earliest written records that West Mayo was called Umhall. Upper Umhall equated with the modern barony of Murrisk, and Lower Umhall with the barony of Burrishoole. The region was inhabited by a powerful clan, the Uí

Briúin (O'Briens), who began to dominate Connacht in the second half of the seventh century. In 787 this tribe was slaughtered by the Uí Fhiachrach (O'Fiachras) of County Sligo, although the O'Briens continued to rule the area for another hundred years. In 913 the area was invaded and devastated by warriors under Niall, king of Ailech in north Donegal.

By the tenth and eleventh centuries new powerful families emerged in Connacht, in particular the O'Conors, O'Flahertys and O'Rorkes. In 1063 it is recorded that during an attack the followers of Hugh O'Conor took refuge in the cave at Aille and 160 people suffocated. It is not certain whether they drowned in the flood waters of the Aille River, which flows through the cave, or were deprived of the air in the cave by their enemy. In 1079 the O'Briens returned with a great army, expelled Rory O'Conor from Connacht and plundered Clew Bay and Croagh Patrick. In 1123 it is recorded that Tadhg

Pl. 36—Clew Bay.

UMHALL

We know that the name of West Mayo at the dawn of history was Umhall (pronounced 'oowel'). This territory was further divided into Upper Umhall and Lower Umhall, which roughly equate with the modern baronies of Murrisk and Burrishoole. It is not known how old this territorial name is or what it means, although since at least the sixteenth century it has been translated from the Irish word *ubhall*, 'apples'. For example, in Grose's *Antiquities of Ireland* (1796), Edward Ledwich explained that the name 'apples' derived from 'the mountains of this country bearing some distant resemblance to this fruit'. However, a more appropriate candidate for the origin of the name may be the islands of Clew Bay at the centre of this region, which resemble apples floating in water.

O'Malley, lord of Umhall, was drowned when his ship sank at Aran. From this period onwards history records the rise of the O'Malleys, who were the dominant family in West Mayo until the sixteenth century.

It was normal custom for the king of a small territory such as Umhall to pay a tribute to the king of Connacht. According to the twelfth-century Book of Rights (*Leabhar na gCeart*), the king of Umhall was obliged to pay the king of Connacht an annual tribute comprising 100 dairy cows, 100 hogs and 100 cloaks. This payment of tribute took place at a ceremony at Rathcroghan in

Pl. 37—Croagh Patrick.

CROAGH PATRICK

'By its very shape, Croagh Patrick was cut out to be a holy mountain...Its sides are gradually seen to narrow symmetrically towards the summit, which is so often shrouded in mist that it could well be imagined as communing with the ancient gods above the clouds. It looks down in a benign yet patriarchal fashion over the drowned drumlins of Clew Bay, which raise their heads above the waves like the whale on which St Brendan's crew landed to light their fire' (Peter Harbison, *Pilgrimage in Ireland*, 1991).

The old Irish name of this mountain was *Crochán Aigli*. According to a medieval text, the mountain was called after Aigle, who was killed here by Crom Derg ('Red Fist'). Before this the mountain was called *Cruachán Gabrois*. The meanings of these two names are not fully understood, although 'Aigle' was frequently mistranslated in the eighteenth century as meaning Eagle Mountain. This was qualified by travel writers such as Richard Pococke, who in 1752 explained it on the grounds 'that it appears like an Eagle stretching out its wings'.

County Roscommon. During the ceremony the tributes from Umhall were made first, and in return the king of Connacht was obliged to pay the king of Umhall 'five steeds, five swords, five ships and five coats of mail'. During the twelfth century the O'Conors had assumed the kingship of Connacht. In 1224, a decade before the arrival of the Anglo-Normans in Connacht, Hugh O'Conor, king of Connacht, was praised in the Annals of Lough Key: 'it was God who granted sovereignty to him thus, for no crime was committed in Connacht…but one act of plunder on the road to Croagh Patrick, and his hands and feet were cut off the person who committed it'.

THE ARRIVAL OF CHRISTIANITY

The earliest Christians arrived in Ireland around 400 years after the birth of Christ. Today we know that Christianity took root gradually and was not immediately as successful as the earliest writings of clerics might suggest. St Patrick has long been associated with the conversion of much of Ireland to Christianity, and he has strong associations with County Mayo. During the sixth century a new generation of Irish clerics, such as St Colum Cille, St Brigid and St Brendan, professed the importance of monastic rule and brought renewed impetus to the Christian church in Ireland. The names of these great saints have been attached to many churches in West Mayo. However, although monasteries and their monks have often symbolised the early Irish church, the bishopric system introduced by St Patrick continued alongside the monasteries.

There is little or no historical evidence to help to identify the earliest churches in West Mayo. The first historical references to churches in the area were made by Bishop Tírechán, who wrote the Life of St Patrick in around 700. His writings record the earliest, perhaps most reliable version of Patrick's visit to the region. According to Tírechán, when St Patrick arrived in West Mayo he went to Aghagower. There he ordained Senachus and gave him a new name, 'Lamb of God'. Senachus requested of Patrick that the church at Aghagower would not be called after his own name. Patrick wrote an alphabet for Senachus's son Óengus. He then consecrated a church there, at the dwelling of Mathona, daughter of Senachus. Patrick said to them: 'there will be good bishops here, and from their seed in this parish there will be blessed people forever'. From here Patrick travelled to Mons Aigli (Croagh Patrick) to fast for forty days and forty nights, following the example of Moses, Elias and Christ. His charioteer Totmael died at Murrisk, on the plain between the sea and the mountain. There Patrick buried Totmael, gathered stones together for his cairn and said: 'So let him be forever; and he will be visited by me at the end of the world.' While on the summit of the mountain, Patrick was tormented by birds gathering towards him so that he could not see the sky or the sea or the land. Then Patrick founded a church somewhere on the plains of West Mayo.

Tírechán was bishop of Armagh in Ulster in around 700 and a native of north Mayo. He attributed many of the churches of his native county to St

Pl. 38—Croagh Patrick.

St Patrick's Bell

Pl. 39—St Patrick's Bell (courtesy of the National Museum of Ireland ©).

Clog Dubh, or the 'Black Bell of St Patrick', was allegedly given to Patrick by St Brigid and was used by him to scatter the demons who tormented him on the summit of Croagh Patrick, becoming cracked in the process. The French tourist de Latocnaye, who travelled around Ireland in 1796–7, was told of 'a black bell for which the inhabitants have a peculiar veneration. It is used as a thing to swear on in legal matters, and no one will dare to perjure himself on it. They...believe that the devil will carry them off immediately if they dare to affirm on it anything that is not true.' Caesar Otway, on his 1838 tour of Connacht, recorded being told by a local man: 'let the man swear what he may upon Gospel or Breviary, when he comes to lay his hand upon the bell he would turn black in the face if he swore anything but the truth'. In 1871 the bell was bought by Sir William Wilde, father of Oscar Wilde, who recorded that 'the pious pilgrim was allowed to kiss it for a penny and if he had been affected by "rheumatic pains", he might put it three times round his body for two pence'. Furthermore, 'It was believed in the locality that this bell was a present from an angel to the saint, and was originally of pure silver, but that it was rendered black and corroded, as at present seen, "by its contact with the demons on Croagh Patrick".'

Pl. 40—Croagh Patrick from Moher Lough.

'DARLING MOUNTAIN...'

'...the darling mountain, the pride, the joy, and the glory of the Connacht peasant' (James Berry, west of Ireland storyteller).

Today pilgrims still come from many parts of the country and the world to make the tortuous climb up Croagh Patrick, sometimes following the old pilgrim route the *Tóchar Phádraig* from Ballintubber Abbey. The mountain is climbed throughout the year, but the main day of pilgrimage is the last Sunday of July (Reek Sunday), a date that reconciles the ancient pagan traditions of Lughnasa with the Christian Sabbath. Thousands of pilgrims climb Croagh Patrick every year, and the path trodden by millions of feet is worn on the slopes of the mountain. Until 1970 the climb to the summit of the mountain itself was frequently performed at night, and even today many venture the stony ascent in bare feet. The mountain has sometimes presented unforeseen dangers, and in 1113 on St Patrick's Day (17 March) thirty pilgrims were killed by lightning on the summit.

During the autumn of 1835 the English traveller John Barrow climbed to the summit and recorded one of the earliest descriptions of pilgrims to the mountain: 'On arriving at the summit we found a poor woman, barefooted and barelegged, her clothing coarse and scanty, trudging seven times round the outer edge of the level summit, which is about an acre, strewed over with small sharp stones, telling her beads [saying the Rosary] as she hopped along...Besides the old woman there were two stray sheep on the summit of Croagh Patrick, who had selected a very bad pasture, as there was not a blade of grass, so that they too were performing penance.'

Patrick, including Aghagower and Croagh Patrick. This may also have been the case with Kilmaclasser, which may have been named after Mac Laisre, abbot of Armagh, who died in 623. Indeed, Kilmaclasser may be the church on the plains of West Mayo that according to Tírechán was founded by Patrick after his visit to Croagh Patrick. Over time the stories of Patrick became increasingly popular and more elaborate, so that today many more churches in the area are also associated with him, including Caher Island, Boheh, Glaspatrick and Furgill. However, it is possible that Patrick never visited the region and that his association with the local churches was invented by Tírechán and others in order to increase the status of these churches by linking them with Armagh, the most powerful church in Ireland, also allegedly founded by Patrick. This was done until quite recent centuries, and a modern graveyard at Oughaval was associated with St Patrick even though the older graveyard there had very strong links with St Colum Cille.

Several churches, in particular Caher Island, appear to have been the hermitage sites of early monks, probably founded in the seventh century. St Colmán, an abbot who succeeded Colum Cille of Iona, as a result of an argument at the famous British monastery of Lindisfarne, left the community there and in 668 founded his own monastery at Inishbofin off the coast of Connemara. Perhaps Colmán or one of his followers also established a foundation on Caher Island and on other islands off the north-western Connacht coastline, following the tradition of Colum Cille, who had founded many island monasteries from his base at Iona in Scotland nearly a century before. It may be no coincidence that there was once a church on the island of Inishturk dedicated to Colum Cille. Also, Oughaval church and holy well are dedicated to Colum Cille. The community founded by St Colmán at Inishbofin consisted of Saxon and Irish monks. However, they were in such a constant state of disagreement that the Saxon monks left Inishbofin and founded their own monastery at Mayo, which has since given its name to the county. On the shores of Islandeady Lough is a church that may derive its name from the Irish *Oileán Éadghair*, 'Edgar's Island'. Edgar is a Saxon name, and he may have been one of the Saxon monks who founded Mayo Abbey.

Some placenames provide interesting clues to the origins of other early churches in the area. For example, churches at Kilbree Upper, Kilbride near Newport, Askillaun near Louisburgh and Capnagower on Clare Island are dedicated to St Brigid of Kildare. The holy wells at Lankill near Aghagower and Roskeen near Burrishoole are dedicated to St Brendan. It seems unlikely that these famous Irish saints founded these early churches themselves, and the names of their original founders and their successors were never recorded.

Another, little-known saint associated with the area is St Marcan, whose church stood at Rosclave, on the shores of Clew Bay south of Newport. In 1838 John O'Donovan of the Ordnance Survey recorded a local legend that when St Brigid paid a visit to St Marcan she was not well received. Enraged, she pronounced a curse, saying 'O little man, the sea shall hereafter come over thy house, and thy fame shall be buried in oblivion, when my life and glorious career shall be published all over the world'. Marcan retorted that there would be a death in her convent every day, to which she replied that such a death would be of a starling. As the early twentieth-century Mayo historian H.T. Knox wrote, 'the only sufferers were the innocent starlings who had to provide corpses'.

The organisation of the Irish church was primarily a monastic one that co-existed with bishops. It was not until the beginning of the twelfth century that the Irish church was gradually reorganised into large dioceses headed by archbishops. Cong in south Mayo became the bishopric for western Connacht in 1111 and was replaced later in that century by Tuam in Galway. At this time Aghagower was the most important church in West Mayo, and the power of this church was probably symbolised by the building of the round tower here in the early twelfth century. On 15 December 1233 the Annals of Connaught record the death of Donn Cathaig, *airchinnech* ('church head') of Aghagower. The annals describe him as 'a man reverenced by clergy and laity for his qualities of mind and body; the most generous bestower of cattle and food in his age; the protector of the wretched and the prosperous; an honour to his land and country; the reconciler of all disputes between his own household and the public in general'.

ARCHAEOLOGY OF THE EARLIEST CHURCHES

In the absence of historical records the earliest church foundations are often difficult to identify. The timber oratories at the centre of these church foundations have long disappeared. However, stone objects from this period have survived, including cross-inscribed slabs, larger pillars and a number of bullaun stones—stone basins that are believed to have been used as early church fonts. Frequently archaeologists must rely on such objects to illustrate the antiquity of a church site. Cross-slabs, such as a range found on Caher Island, as well as at Boheh, Kilgeever and Knappaghmanagh, appear to date to the seventh and eighth centuries. There are also series of tall pillar stones with inscribed crosses found at Cloonlaur, Dadreen, Doughmakeon and Lankill. Bullaun stones occur at Fahburren, Furgill, Carrowkennedy, Kilbride and Lankill. These bullaun stones, cross-slabs and pillars indicate a large number of early monastic foundations throughout West Mayo in the seventh and eighth centuries.

During the early period timber was the most common raw material used in the construction of church buildings, and consequently these buildings do not survive today. From around AD 900 stone began to be used more widely to build churches, and some of these buildings survive. These were typically small rectangular buildings. At the east end a window in the east gable, and sometimes the south wall, provided light for the altar. The door was most commonly situated at the west end of the church. These doors typically had flat

Pl. 41—Caher Island cross-slab.

Pls 42 and 43—Caher Island cross-slabs.

OILEÁN NA NAOMH

On Caher Island near Inishturk are the remains of a beautiful monastic site, featuring many cross-slabs believed to date to the seventh or eighth century. The island is also known in Irish as *Oileán na Naomh*, 'the blessed island'. The sanctity of the island has always been highly respected, and at the beginning of the nineteenth century passing fishermen would raise their hats and say a prayer in Irish: *Umhluímíd do Dhia mhór na huile chomhachta agus do Phádraig míorbhúilteach* ('We make reverence to the great, all-powerful God and to Patrick the miracle worker'). Pilgrims still come on 15 August, and at one time pilgrimage to Croagh Patrick on Reek Sunday was only properly completed by a visit to Caher Island.

A seventh-century cross-slab (far left) near the church ruins on Caher Island has an interesting feature known as a chi-rho monogram. The hook protruding from the top left of the cross represents the loop of the letter 'P', sometimes used to symbolise the Greek initial of Christ's name. It has been suggested that the trio of boxed bosses below the cross represent the Trinity.

Pl. 44—Leac na Naomh, on Caher Island.

Leac na Naomh

In 1838 John O'Donovan of the Ordnance Survey wrote: 'St. Patrick and his contemporary saints impressed this flag with a degree of sanctity, which the rain, storms and improvements of 1500 years have been unable to remove'. O'Donovan was told that the stone was once used by locals 'to elicit the truth' if they were 'aggrieved or scandalised openly and wrongfully...They first fast and pray at home for a fixed time, imploring that God, through the intercession of St. Patrick and the other saints who blessed this flag, would bring about some occurrence, which would shew that they were wronged on such occasions, and after the fasting and praying are over, they sail over to Caher and turn Leac na Naomh. After this flag is turned, the weather immediately becomes unfavourable...and some event is, ere long, brought about, which shews clearly to the eyes of all the neighbours, that the character of the person who turned the Leac, had unjustly and wrongfully attempted to be blackened. This may be shewn in various ways, such as some great misfortune happening to the scandaliser, or in the case of the theft, the real thief being discovered.'

On 6 January 1839 a great wind stormed across Ireland, an event that became known throughout the country as the 'Night of the Big Wind'. Later that year Caesar Otway, in his *Tour of Connaught,* wrote that the storm was supposedly caused by a woman from Murrisk who had turned Leac na Naomh 'with a fearful malediction on her neighbours. I suppose she did not consider how much good she was about to do with her ill wind when it brought *luck* to all the slaters, sawyers, glaziers, &c. &c. in Ireland.'

Fig. 11—Cross-slab from Feenune near Killadoon.

Fig. 12—Lankill cross pillar (after Herity 1995b).

This cross-inscribed pillar marks the site of an early church at Lankill near Aghagower. The stone is probably a prehistoric standing stone that has been Christianised with this elaborate cross.

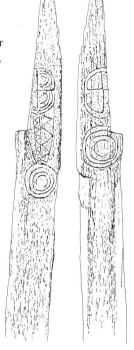

KNAPPAGHMANAGH CROSS-SLAB

One of the most unusual cross-slabs in Ireland is from Knappaghmanagh (*Cnapan na manach*, 'hilly land of the monks'). The cross occurs within a circle that forms the body of a human figure. The precise meaning of this is not truly understood. While the figure may represent Christ, it does not appear to represent the Crucifixion.

Pl. 45—Knappaghmanagh cross-slab.

*Pl. 46
Cloonlaur
cross-slab.*

CLOONLAUR CROSS-SLAB AND PILLAR

This small cross-slab and seventh-century cross-inscribed pillar are the only remnants of an early church at Killeen, which probably gave its name to the neighbouring townland of Killadoon. The great west of Ireland storyteller James Berry recorded that the church once had 'a privilege not enjoyed by any other church in Christendom…The privilege, as contained in tradition, is that no matter what crime a person has been found guilty of, even murder, if he escaped and ran to the church of Killeen and placed one of his fingers in the keyhole of the church door, he would be let go free.' The cross-slab appears to show crosses with handles, perhaps processional crosses. The pillar has a Maltese cross with a tulip design.

*Pl. 47
Cloonlaur
cross
pillar.*

DOUGHMAKEON MALTESE CROSS

In the sand dunes at Doughmakeon is a stone pillar decorated with a Maltese cross, an early form of cross used in Ireland. This example appears to mark the site of a church now submerged beneath the sands of time. In around the middle of the nineteenth century the stone was found buried in the sands and was re-erected where it now stands. This may be the stone, recorded by John O'Donovan of the Ordnance Survey in 1838, that stood on the shores of nearby Lough Cahasy, which was known as *Claidhimhín Chathasaigh*, 'Cathansach's little sword'. He went on to say: 'Long may it be drawn in defense of honest fame, and

*Pl. 48—
Doughmakeon
Maltese cross.*

may no modern unbeliever blunt its edge until he establishes the force of morality on such a firm basis as to need its aid no longer'. The stone was used as a cursing stone, and Caesar Otway in 1838 was told by the servant of the Revd Charles Seymour from Louisburgh of 'the stone of Duac McShaun—this was a flag on the sandy shore south-west of the Old Head…"You may be sure," says he, "that during the harvest this flag is well watched—good care is taken that nobody shall PLAY THE DEVIL at that time"…It was sometime ago stolen away by a man notorious for his evil deeds, and thrown by night into the deep sea; he thereby thought to avoid the ruin that those whom he had injured might bring on him by turning the stone, and invoking its curse against him. The ruffian, however, did not escape; his victims went, and when they found the flag gone, they turned the sand, and the fellow died like a poisoned rat.' There may be some truth in the stories that tell of its destruction; however, it seems that the guilty party, perhaps out of superstition, had the stone buried beneath the sand rather than broken up and thrown into the ocean.

At a graveyard at Fahburren is a bullaun stone, an Early Christian holy water font.

Pl. 49—Fahburren bullaun stone.

lintels across the top, and their jambs inclined slightly towards the top. An example of this type of door survives at Oughaval, although the rest of the building is of a later date. This appears to be the only example of early church architecture surviving in West Mayo. At the turn of the twelfth century a new style called Romanesque was introduced to Ireland. This form of architecture is characterised by the use of round arches in the construction of windows, doorways and to divide the nave from the chancel of a church. In a few rare examples these arches are highly decorated; however, the few examples in West Mayo are quite plain. For example, at Aghagower is a plain but finely carved arched doorway. The east window of the church at Kilgeever is typical of the simple round-headed windows that were favoured in much of Ireland during the twelfth century.

The early churches may have been simple buildings, but we know that the earliest stonemasons were competent at their trade from their achievements in the building of round towers at some churches, such as Aghagower. These magnificent towers were designed not as blatantly obvious buildings in which to hide from would-be attackers (although they were used as places of refuge on occasion) but as belfries. However, they were not intended as ordinary bell towers but were designed to symbolise the power and achievements of the

*Pl. 50—
Doorway of
church at
Oughaval.*

DOORWAYS

At Oughaval is a square-headed doorway of a late eleventh- or early twelfth-century church, the earliest surviving piece of church architecture in the area. This may be the doorway into the church in which it is recorded in the Annals of Ulster that a member of the O'Malley family was slain by the son of Donnell O'Dowda in 1131. O'Dowda was killed three months later by his own spear 'through the miracle of Columcille'. John O'Donovan, who visited the site in 1838, met an elderly man who told him of a stone here called *Leac Cholumb Cille*, to which people turned to wish each other bad luck but which had been broken by order of the priest in the eighteenth century. Outside the graveyard is a dried-up holy well dedicated to St Colum Cille.

The simple round-headed doorway at Aghagower dates from the end of the twelfth century and represents a revolutionary form of church architecture in Ireland known as Romanesque. In its simplest form this style of architecture employed round arches for windows and doorways. Close examination of the stones reveals the diagonal toolmarks typical of late twelfth-century stonemasons.

*Pl. 51—
Doorway of
church at
Aghagower.*

church. At the time these were the tallest buildings in Ireland, towering above anything previously built by a bishop or a king. Indeed, many round towers were built with the financial assistance and patronage of a local king. These towers soared towards heaven and symbolised the links with God that only the church could achieve. The round tower at Aghagower was also an impressive landmark to the pilgrims approaching the church as they made their way to Croagh Patrick. The fact that this and many other round towers remain standing and virtually intact today is a testimony to the skills of the masons who designed and built them some 900 years ago.

Relics were frequently kept at these early churches. Near Aghagower are the ruins of a small church known as *Teampull na bhFiacal*, 'the church of the tooth'. There is a tradition that St Patrick lost his last tooth on Croagh Patrick and left it with a bishop at Aghagower. It appears that a relic of St Patrick's tooth was stored at this church and was probably venerated by pilgrims who travelled along the *Tóchar Phádraig*, the pilgrim road that passes beside the church ruins. The most famous relic is the Black Bell of St Patrick, which was traditionally brought to the summit of Croagh Patrick on Reek Sunday for veneration by pilgrims. In the nineteenth century the bell was in the custodianship of a family called Geraghty, who claimed to be its hereditary stewards.

*Pl. 52—
Gaming-piece
from Tallavbaun
(courtesy of the
National
Museum of
Ireland ©).*

GAMING-PIECE

On the white sands of Tallavbaun are the remains of a church that has been all but washed away by the high tides and winds coming in from the Atlantic Ocean. There is a tradition that a bell was once found at this church, but it has since been lost. However, still surviving in the National Museum of Ireland are a steatite spindle whorl and a gaming-piece found at this site, both objects probably dating to around 900. The bone gaming-piece is a disc *c.* 4cm across, decorated on one side with an elaborate compass-drawn design. The spindle whorl may highlight the mundane jobs carried out by the monks, and the gaming-piece may illustrate a more lighthearted aspect to their lifestyle.

ROUND TOWERS

At Aghagower is a fine example of a round tower, a tall, majestic belfry with a twelfth-century round-headed doorway. We will never know how tall this tower once stood: like many others around the country, it was severely damaged by lightning, at the beginning of the nineteenth century, and the capstone is supposed to have landed on the nearby hill of Tevenish. There is a tradition that the bell is buried in a nearby bog known as Knockadooge, where people used to hear it 'giving tongue'.

These were primarily bell towers; however, they were occasionally used as a place of refuge during attack on the monastery. The tower at Aghagower appears to have been used in such a way at one time: the doorway shows cracks from intense burning, perhaps in an attempt to dislodge whomever had taken refuge inside.

Many fanciful theories have been suggested for round towers. Perhaps the wildest was put forward by the eighteenth-century antiquarian General Vallency. He argued that 'Agha Gower' meant 'Fire of Fires' and used this to show that round towers were pre-Christian fire temples. In 1838 the great scholar of the Irish language John O'Donovan showed that the name derives from the Irish *Achaidh fobhair*, 'field of the spring'. O'Donovan concluded with sarcasm that 'when Aghagower does not mean fire of fires, nor water of water, nor ass of asses, where is the *vis consequential*?'.

The consecrated ground around early churches was enclosed by a circular wall of earth and stone. Most of these enclosures do not survive; however, a fine example can still be seen at Knappaghmanagh. The cross-inscribed pillar at Dadreen was associated with a large oval enclosure known as Caheravilla, *Cathrach a bhile,* 'stone fort of the sacred tree'. There is no trace of the enclosure or the sacred tree at Dadreen, but it is known that a sacred tree, or *bile,* was a common feature of early Irish monasteries. Today the peaceful ruins and graveyards of these early churches disguise what were originally busy centres of learning, crafts and industry. They depended largely on patronage from the local rulers, and, given the large number of church sites in the area, there must have been a wealthy population living there at this time.

Holy wells are found near many church sites, and the church at Aghagower takes its name from the Irish *Achaidh fobhair,* meaning 'field of the spring well'. These wells, like the saints to whom they are dedicated, are frequently

Pl. 54— Dadreen cross pillar.

Sometimes a cross was inscribed on a large stone pillar that may have marked the consecrated bounds of a church. This cross pillar at Dadreen is all that remains of a church here. It may originally have been a pagan standing stone, reused and Christianised during the seventh century with the carving of this cross.

associated with healing. In 1838 John O'Donovan of the Ordnance Survey recorded a local tradition that the well at Oughaval 'contains three blessed trouts, which are great pets with the pilgrims, to whom they always appear when the waters of the well are about to afford relief, but should a pilgrim be incurable, it is said they always hide themselves at the bottom of the well'. Also in that year, Caesar Otway was told a story of 'how some Protestant had carried the fish home and placed it to fry on a gridiron for his dinner; but that the fish bounded, and why should it not? *off* the iron, *out* of the kitchen, *over* the fields, and never stopped until it was safe and cool swimming in the well'. Thereafter the trout had the marks of the hot bars on its side. Near Burrishoole is Tobernasool (*Tobar na súl*, 'well of the eyes'), the water of which is said to cure eye ailments. The well at Capnagower on Clare Island is known locally as Toberfelabride (*Tobar Féile Bríd*, 'the well of Brigid's festival'), although stations were performed here not on the saint's day but on 15 August (the Feast of the Assumption). In 1911 the antiquarian Thomas Westropp wrote that 'the well is accredited with many miracles of healing, even in recent years', and he recorded a local story of how a delicate boy who had been too feeble to walk was cured.

DEFENDED SETTLEMENTS

Outside monasteries, wealthy farmers built defended ringforts or stone cashels around their farmsteads. These consisted of a circular bank or stone wall surrounded by a ditch. The farmhouse, often round in plan, lay within this ringfort or cashel. Archaeological excavations elsewhere in Ireland have shown that a number of the larger sites, presumably belonging to the wealthiest landowners, had metal and glass workshops within. It is not clear why it was necessary to construct a ringfort around these farmsteads, especially given that a single bank or ditch would only have provided a token deterrent against would-be attackers. Therefore, it seems that the defences were more symbolic than practical. Ringforts are perhaps the most common archaeological monument surviving in the landscape today, and their widespread distribution indicates a relatively high rural population during the early medieval period. West Mayo has many examples of ringforts and cashels. Ringforts are typically found on the drumlin hills of the eastern shores of Clew Bay, between Westport and Newport, and cashels are more commonly found on stony ground, particularly on mountainous slopes. Many ringforts survived in the landscape because they were believed by later generations to be the abodes of fairies. This is preserved in the Irish name *Lios a phúca*, 'the fort of the ghost', of a ringfort at Letterbrock near Carrowkennedy, south of Westport.

In the north of Umhall at Letterkeen is a ringfort known locally as *Lios na Gaoithe*, 'the windy fort', which was excavated by Seán Ó Ríordáin and Máire MacDermott in 1950. It is very similar to other ringforts in the area, and the excavations provided important evidence of the structure and use of these sites.

Fig. 13—Polished stone axe from Rostoohy.

This Stone Age polished stone axe was found a short distance from the ringfort at Rostoohy, and it was reported that several more were found in the same field. Indeed, the name Rostoohy may derive from the Irish words *ros* ('headland') and *tuadh* ('axes'). Several such axes have been found at other Irish ringforts, and it has been argued that they were deliberately collected and reused during the early medieval period for polishing woven cloth. Part of a stone axe and several rounded stones found during the excavations at Letterkeen ringfort may have been used for a similar purpose.

The site originally consisted of a water-filled ditch enclosing a high bank. At the entrance were several post-holes, in which the timber uprights had been placed to support a wooden gate structure. Sometime later a souterrain was dug inside the entrance, and the spoil from this was used to build a causeway across the ditch. At this time a bank was constructed around the entire site and a timber fence was erected on it. This fence enclosed the site and lined either side of the causeway that crossed the ditch. Inside the fort was evidence for a circular timber house and a corn-drying kiln. In the nearby ashes were fragments of a rotary quern, which would have been used to grind the corn. At one place was an area of intense burning and a few fragments of crucible, perhaps the

JEWELLERY

Only a relatively small number of artefacts were found during the excavations of a ringfort at Letterkeen. Among them were a bronze ring-pin, two glass beads, a glass bracelet and two portions of jet bracelets. These provide an insight into the jewellery fashions of the time. Such objects could only be afforded by the wealthy of the day, indicating the status of the inhabitants of this ringfort.

Pl. 56— Selection of artefacts from Letterkeen ringfort (courtesy of the National Museum of Ireland ©).

Pl. 57—Promontory fort on Lough Feeagh.

PROMONTORY FORTS

Occasionally a promontory on the coastline or in a lake, as in this case extending into Lough Feeagh, was defended by fortifying a narrow neck of land with a stone wall or earthen bank near the mainland. The promontory was naturally defended by water on the other three sides, and anyone attacking this fort could only gain access at one narrow point.

Pl. 58—Knappaghbeg Lough crannog.

CRANNOGS

Occasionally wealthy landowners of this period built artificial islands in lakes. Their location made access to them more difficult, and they must have been used as places of refuge during times of trouble. They may also have been places where craftsmen, commissioned by the local chieftain, produced valuable metal or glass objects in safety. This crannog at the north end of Knappaghbeg Lough near Westport is small, and there are much larger examples at Moher Lough and Ballin Lough.

VIKING HOARD

The Vikings, when they first arrived in Ireland at the close of the eighth century, specialised in raiding vulnerable but wealthy churches, such as Inishbofin off the Connemara coast in 795. It appears that the Vikings landed in Clew Bay in 812, perhaps to set up camp for the winter; however, it is recorded that they were slaughtered by the local tribes. In the following year the Vikings returned, and this time they took revenge, killing the local king, Coscrach. In 1939 a hoard of 25 silver bracelets was found at Cushalogurt, on the eastern shores of Clew Bay. These have been dated to the end of the tenth century and may represent trading between the local Irish and the Viking settlers.

Pl. 59—Viking hoard found at Cushalogurt, Kilmeena (courtesy of the National Museum of Ireland ©).

remains of a metal workshop.

Many ringforts and cashels have a souterrian, frequently known to local people as a 'cave'. The term souterrain derives from the French *sous* (under) and *terrain* (ground) to describe an underground passageway. At Letterkeen is a souterrain consisting of a simple passageway 9m long and over 1m wide. There was no evidence for roof stones, and it seems to have been roofed with timber, suggesting that it was used for storage, for example to keep food cool. A similar souterrain, but with drystone walling and a stone roof, occurs within a cashel at Durless. However, other souterrains were much more elaborate and contained hidden passageways and chambers, such as at Knappaghmanagh. These chambers were frequently provided with air vents and were designed as places of temporary refuge during a raid.

Wealthy landowners also built crannogs, artificial lake islands, such as at Moher Lough and Ballin Lough, which could only be reached by boat. The term derives from the Irish words *crann* ('tree') and *óg* ('young'), reflecting the large amounts of timber used in the construction of their surrounding palisade and internal houses. These were damp, uncomfortable places in which to live and may have been used only in the summer months or during troubled times. Crannogs were most commonly used in the seventh century, but it is known that many others were built as early as the Bronze Age and the Iron Age, and others were used during the Tudor Conquest of Ireland in the final years of the sixteenth century.

Pl. 60—Knappaghmore cashel.

The late Middle Ages

THE ANGLO-NORMAN CONQUEST

Pl. 61—Detail of a wall painting in Clare Island Abbey showing a knight on horseback.

During the twelfth century Ireland had established many political and economic links with European neighbours, in particular Britain. In 1169 a large number of Anglo-Norman knights and soldiers came from England and Wales to Ireland as mercenaries to Diarmait MacMurrough, the Leinster king who had been dethroned by Rory O'Conor, king of Connacht and high king of Ireland. At this time the O'Malleys ruled West Mayo, or Umhall as it was then known, and it is recorded that Donnell O'Malley, lord of Umhall, died in 1177. The Anglo-Normans had conquered much of Ireland by the time they encamped near Aghagower in 1230, where they were met by Manus O'Conor, who submitted to them. Four years later the Anglo-Normans attempted a total conquest of western Connacht.

An Anglo-Norman army led by Richard de Burgh (Burke) arrived in West Mayo in 1235 and fought a naval battle in Clew Bay against Manus O'Conor, who was aided by the O'Flahertys from Connemara. The O'Conors were on Inis Aonaigh and Inis Raithin. However, the Anglo-Normans took their boats to the shore at Bartraw and loaded them with a large, well-armed, mail-clad army, who

58

In 1235 the Anglo-Normans came to Clew Bay and fought a naval battle with Manus O'Conor, who was aided by the O'Flahertys from Connemara. During the battle, which the Anglo-Normans won, the local O'Malley clan remained neutral, and soon after the battle two sons of the local king, Muiredach O'Malley, were killed in revenge by the O'Conors on Clare Island, seen here in the distance.

landed on the islands, killing all they found there. The O'Conors fled, and the Anglo-Normans took all the cattle from the islands. The annals make it clear that the O'Conors were not friendly with the O'Malleys, who would otherwise have joined them. Later in the year Donnell O'Conor, son of Manus O'Conor, killed Donnell and Murtough O'Malley on Clare Island, perhaps in revenge for their staying neutral in the previous battle.

Pl. 62— Clew Bay and Clare Island.

Those Anglo-Norman knights who helped in the Conquest were granted lands in the newly gained territory. Among these was Henry Butler, who established a manor at Burrishoole, where he built a castle. However, one of the problems faced by the Anglo-Normans in this area was that they settled here only in small numbers, and Henry Butler, as lord of his manor, was largely absent from his estate. This made consolidation and defence of the lands extremely difficult, and the Butler castle at Burrishoole was burned by the O'Conors (including the sons of Manus) in 1248, with the spoils taken to the islands in Clew Bay. Shortly afterwards the Anglo-Normans under John D'Exeter, John Butler and Robin Lawless marched to Aghagower and plundered the region. They were followed by Henry Butler, who came to

Umhall with his own army to defend his castle and manor, and engaged in another battle in Clew Bay with the O'Conors. In the battle Diarmait, son of Manus O'Conor, was killed. In 1272 Henry Butler and his chief lieutentant, Hosty Merrick, were killed by the O'Conors (including Cathal O'Conor, son of Conor Roe). However, the following year the Anglo-Normans returned and expelled the O'Conors.

When the Anglo-Normans took control of a region, their castles generally consisted of a keep (the lord's residence) surrounded by a bawn wall forming a defended courtyard around it. These castles allowed the Anglo-Normans to centralise their power and administration and were also intended to be symbolic of power. However, the design of the castles was always practical, based on the need to make them impenetrable. Such castles were built at Doon, east of Westport, and at Burrishoole, but there is little to be seen at these sites today. Apart from the Butlers, we know very little about the earliest Anglo-Norman settlers in the area, although it seems that the Burkes may have arrived here at this stage. Elsewhere these settlers built fortifications, frequently stone castles, but, apart from the remains near Burrishoole and at Doon, the other castles are not recorded in history or folk tradition. However, there are occasional earthwork sites from this period that are somewhat different from the earlier ringforts. One example of these is a raised platform overlooking a stream at Drumgoney in Kilmaclasser. This would originally have been a timber fortification with a timber tower inside. This castle may have been replaced in the fifteenth century by a nearby tower-house at Brokagh built by the Clan Gibbons.

If we know very little about where the Anglo-Normans built their castles, we know even less about where the Irish lived at this time. The Anglo-Norman commentator Gerald de Barry, writing at the end of the twelfth century, declared that the 'Irish attach no importance to castles, they make the woods their strong-hold and the bogs their trenches'. It appears that the Irish did not conform to the Anglo-Norman methods of warfare, which were largely dependent on castles. Instead, the native Irish may have continued to live in the ringforts, cashels and crannogs of their predecessors. In warfare the Irish used the natural defences of the landscape rather than a fixed fortification such as a castle. This reduced the impact of the Anglo-Norman armoured knights and archers, who preferred to undertake an open battle or siege of a castle.

THE O'MALLEYS AND THE GAELIC REVIVAL

The Anglo-Norman Conquest of west Connacht was flawed at very basic levels, and there was no long-term strategy to consolidate the territory won or to defend it from the native Gaelic chieftains. During the early fourteenth century the Gaelic chieftains began to find weaknesses in the Anglo-Norman settlement. These weaknesses were accentuated by a number of events, including the Bruce Invasion of Ireland in 1316 and the Black Death, a plague that had catastrophic effects on Anglo-Norman-controlled urban centres such as Dublin. These events diminished the effectiveness of the Anglo-Norman administration in Ireland, and the Gaelic chieftains quickly took advantage for their own goals. In 1333 John Butler still held the castle at Burrishoole; however, it seems that soon afterwards the Butlers were forced to leave their castle and, while they retained ownership of the land, they never again lived in the area or received rents from their tenants there.

This period saw the rise to new heights of power of the seafaring O'Malley clan of Murrisk and Clare Island. The poet O'Dugan, who died in 1372, wrote:

> A good man never there was
> of the Ui Mhaille [O'Malleys], but a mariner
> Of every weather they are prophets
> A tribe of brotherly affection and of friendship.

POWERFUL BY LAND AND SEA

In the ruins of the abbey on Clare Island is a stone plaque with the O'Malley coat of arms, featuring a stallion surmounting a helmet, which is in turn above a boar—a symbol of warriors. The boar is surrounded by three bows with arrows pointing at it. Beneath the boar is a galley and an inscription featuring the name O'Maille (O'Malley) and the Latin motto *Terra marique potens* ('Powerful by land and sea').

Fig. 14—The O'Malley coat of arms.

The O'Malleys earned a reputation as ruthless pirates and terrorised shipping to and from Galway town. They were also highly involved in legal trade between the west coast of Ireland and the coastal areas of France and, in particular, Spain. They ruled the southern shores of Clew Bay unopposed for over 300 years. In the words of a fifteenth-century poem:

> They are the lions of the green sea
> Men acquainted with the land of Spain
> When seizing cattle from Cantyre,
> A mile by sea is a short distance to the O'Malleys.

In 1401 it is recorded that Domnall O'Malley, king of Umhall, died. In 1415 there was conflict within the O'Malley family, when Hugh O'Malley, king of Umhall, fought Diarmait O'Malley, head of another family branch. In the battle Diarmait fled to Clare Island but was pursued by Hugh. The scribe of the Annals of Connaught wrote: 'by Heaven it would have been better for them if they had not met anymore'. In the final battle many members of each family died, including Hugh O'Malley himself and his eldest son Conor, and the kingship was transferred to Diarmait, who had lost his own son Donnell in the battle. Little else is known about the battle, but it seems to have had a devastating effect on the O'Malley lineage. This may be the origin of the folk stories about the water of the holy well at Moyna in Kilmeena, which was allegedly used to change the sex of an O'Malley baby girl to a boy in order to preserve the O'Malley lineage following the slaughter of the O'Malley men on Clare Island.

Another powerful family in Connacht was the O'Flahertys of neighbouring County Galway, and they frequently, though not always, allied themselves with the O'Malleys. It is recorded that in 1417 eighteen members of the O'Flaherty family were drowned in Clew Bay. It is not known why they were in Clew Bay, but perhaps they had perceived a weakness in the O'Malleys since the internal conflicts in that family two years earlier and were attempting to expand their influence into this area. The de Burgo (Burke) family were Anglo-Normans who had settled lands around Burrishoole during the initial invasion of the mid-thirteenth century. One hundred years or so later the Burkes renounced their allegiance to the English monarchy and were incorporated into the Gaelic way of life, becoming 'more Irish than the Irish themselves'. In the fifteenth century, and possibly even earlier, the Burkes had become close allies of the native Gaelic O'Malley clan. This allegiance was probably reinforced by marriage, for example of Thomas Burke to Gráinne O'Malley, who donated a silver chalice to Burrishoole Abbey in 1494. Other families that came to prominence during this period were the MacGibbons, the MacPhilbins and the MacTibbots, all septs of the Burke clan. In 1351 the MacPhilbins took Hugh O'Rourke, lord of Breifny, prisoner on his return from pilgrimage to Croagh Patrick. In revenge the MacDermots of Sligo, allies of O'Rourke, attacked the

MacPhilbins, and the battle resulted in heavy losses on both sides.

Tower-houses are a form of castle that was popular among the ruling Irish chieftains of Connacht in the fifteenth century and can be found at Castleaffy, Rockfleet and Clare Island. They differ from castles in that they were intended to serve more as a fortified residence than a self-sufficient, garrisoned fortress. Tower-houses were often designed to a standard plan: rectangular, three storeys high, with a vault over the ground floor, and topped by a steeply pitched slate or thatch roof. The roof was protected by a battlemented parapet, sometimes featuring a machicolation, which projects or overhangs the parapet directly above the doorway so that objects could safely be dropped on attackers. Within the thickness of the wall were staircase passages and other features such as garderobes (medieval toilets). Windows were small in order to retain heat and keep out damp, but these would still have been dark and cold places in which to live. Only a few tower-houses survive today, but we know from seventeenth-century documents that they were originally more widespread. These

Pl. 63—Rockfleet tower-house.

ROCKFLEET TOWER-HOUSE

Tower-houses were built in the fifteenth century as the fortified residences of wealthy landowners. Several were sited along the shores of Clew Bay to defend the secluded harbours of fleets, hence the name Rockfleet, a direct translation of the old Irish name for the castle, Carrigahowley, *Carraig an Chobhlaigh*. This tower-house was the chief residence of the Burke family of West Mayo.

*Pl. 64—
Clare Island
tower-house,
built by the
O'Malleys.*

Pl. 65—Castleaffy tower-house.

Guarding a now-peaceful inlet of Clew Bay is a tower-house, probably built by a branch of the Burke family known as the MacTibbots. The ruins provide a convenient cross-section of a typical tower-house, showing a vaulted ceiling at first-floor level and passages within the thickness of the walls.

documents also describe features that were originally attached to such tower-houses but have not survived to the present day. These include bawn walls, which effectively defended a courtyard around the castle; such a bawn still survives at MacPhilbins' castle at Toberrooaun near Aghagower. Some also had barbicans, which were defended entrances to the castles. Usually these castles had small villages nearby, and it is known that several had mills attached to them. During the many power struggles of the fifteenth and sixteenth centuries, the Burkes and their family septs frequently hired mercenary soldiers called gallowglasses. In the seventeenth century there was a portion of land in Carraholly, near the site of Bawn Castle, called *Cregean na golloglagh*, 'the rocky land of the gallowglasses'.

The Butler castle at Burrishoole appears to have fallen out of use in the fourteenth century. Of the castles that existed in the fifteenth and sixteenth centuries, few have survived to the present day, and many were in poor condition by the seventeenth century. Originally the area had many more fortifications than the surviving evidence might suggest. The O'Malleys held castles at Cahernamart (Westport), Belclare, Carrowmore and Clare Island; the Burkes at Rockfleet, Ballyviaghan (Newport) and Carrickaneady nearby; the MacPhilbins at Doon, Ballyknock and Toberrooaun; the MacGibbons at Ballyknock; and the MacTibbots at Castleaffy.

NEW MONASTIC ORDERS AND CHURCHES

Many churches had fallen out of use before the Anglo-Normans arrived in West Mayo. Those that survived were generally patronised by the local chieftain and frequently developed into parish churches, such as Aghagower, Islandeady, Kilgeever, Kilmeena, Kilmaclasser and Oughaval. In some cases entirely new churches were built, especially in the fifteenth century, for example Islandeady. In other instances older churches were modified with the incorporation of new, Gothic-style windows or doors, such as the door at Kilgeever. Gothic architecture of churches and abbeys sometimes consisted of quite simple pointed arches but was often very decorative, with carved human heads and floral designs.

The Continental orders of friars and monks, in particular the Augustinians and Cistercians, first arrived in Ireland in the twelfth century. The church on Clare Island was attached to the Cistercian abbey at Abbeyknockmoy in Galway. By 1400 many of the monks in the Gaelic areas of Ireland such as Mayo had abandoned the normal rules of monastic life and had openly married. Irish monasteries became increasingly secularised, and the Cistercians, who had previously dominated the monastic scene, were in decline. However, a new dynamism was injected into the monastic orders towards the end of the fifteenth century, when the Augustinians founded Murrisk Abbey and the Dominicans founded Burrishoole Abbey. The Augustinians and Dominicans followed less stringent regimes than the Cistercians, and this more flexible approach allowed them more direct participation in a variety of pastoral

Pl. 66—Sheela-na-gig at Aghagower.
Built into the wall of Dabhach Patrick ('Patrick's Bath'), facing the village pub, is a small 'sheela-na-gig'. The carving is an explicit portrait of a female figure. This stone was probably originally built into the nearby church, perhaps in the west or south wall, where it could be clearly seen by visitors to the church. It would have acted as a warning against the evils of lust.

Pl. 67—Carved head at Aghagower.
A carved head on the mullion of the east window at Aghagower church may have kept a watchful eye over the altar that would have stood below the window.

Pl. 68—Islandeady church.

Pl. 70—Base of mullion of east window at Islandeady church.

Pl. 69—East window of Islandeady church.

ISLANDEADY CHURCH

On the shores of Islandeady Lough is the church of Islandeady, a fine example of a simple fifteenth-century church with some elaborate decorative features. The ogee-headed window in the west gable is typical of the period, and the door in the south wall is quite elaborate for such a small church. The east window is attractively carved with some fine decorative details. For example, at the base of the mullion are some very small carved details, including two crosses, a triquetra knot (sometimes used as a symbol of the Trinity) and a unique representation of an elaborate tracery window, not unlike the east window at Murrisk Abbey. The technical term for this form of window is switch-line tracery, and it consists of curving arcs that cross over each other like railway tracks.

BURRISHOOLE ABBEY

The beautiful Dominican friary of Burrishoole, dedicated to St Mary, was founded in 1470 by Richard de Burgo, who entered the order himself and lived there until his death in 1473. Permission from the Pope was not sought for the foundation of the abbey, an oversight for which the community faced a threat of excommunication; however, in 1486 Pope Innocent VIII instructed the archbishop of Tuam to grant the friars absolution.

Pl. 71—Burrishoole Abbey.

This fifteenth-century bronze seal matrix was found in 1916 embedded in a window of the upstairs dormitory at Burrishoole Abbey. The seal features a bareheaded figure wearing a cloak and holding a staff surmounted by a cross. The figure stands in a niche in the shape of a trefoil-headed window, typical of contemporary churches, and there are several examples at Burrishoole. The inscription does not mention the friary by name, but it was probably used as the seal of the friary in any correspondence or documentation.

Fig. 15—Burrishoole seal matrix (after Armstrong 1917).

Pl. 72—Burrishoole Abbey c. 1890 (courtesy of Gary Wynne ©).

HOLY BONES

Mr and Mrs S.C. Hall recorded an incredible story during their tour of Ireland in 1842 that indicates the reverence with which local people held the bones of the monks at Burrishoole Abbey: 'At Burrishoole, there was pointed out to us a recess, in which the collected bones are believed to be those of the monks. The skulls contained here are regarded with especial veneration; and, even now, it is by no means uncommon for the peasantry to borrow one of them, when a member of the family is sick, and to boil milk in it which is given to the sufferer, as an infallible cure; the skull, when the object has been answered, is carefully restored to the heap. We examined several that had external marks of fire; and all our doubts upon the subject were removed, for a woman actually came while we were speculating concerning the matter, took a fragment of one away in her apron, and in reply to our questions, did not hesitate to assure us of her conviction that the draught so prepared would cure "her poor babby"'.

DE BURGO–O'MALLEY CHALICE

This silver gilt chalice is only 23cm high and is perhaps the finest example of a fifteenth-century chalice in Ireland. The octagonal stem has a knop with diamond-shaped projections with blue and green enamel insets. Underneath the base of the chalice is a Latin inscription:

Thomas de Burgo et Grania Ni Malle me fieri fecerunt Anno Domini MCCCCLXXXXIIII.

Thomas de Burgo and Grania Ni Malle caused me to be made A.D. 1494.

Thomas de Burgo (Burke, who was also known as Crosach, meaning 'scarred'), who commissioned the chalice, was the grandson of Richard Bourke, the founder of Burrishoole Abbey, and it has been suggested that the chalice was made for the monks there. Thomas Burke's wife, Gráinne O'Malley, is probably a great-grandaunt of the more famous Gráinne (Grace) O'Malley, alias Granuaile.

Pl. 73—De Burgo–O'Malley Chalice (courtesy of the National Museum of Ireland ©).

activities in parishes, hospitals and schools.

Unlike the earlier Irish monastery, with its churches and domestic buildings scattered haphazardly, the medieval abbey was designed as an all-in-one building, containing the church, cloister, kitchen, refectory and dormitory under one roof. The structured nature of the architecture and layout of these buildings reflects the structured lives of the monks. Often the architecture is elaborate and deliberately imposing, for example featuring Gothic-style windows and carved human heads keeping a watchful eye on the outside world. Today we perceive these buildings to have been dark and grey. However, they were originally quite colourful, particularly internally, and the wall paintings that survive within the church on Clare Island clearly show how highly decorated some were.

By 1540 Henry VIII, the newly appointed head of the Church of Ireland under the Protestant Reformation, had dissolved the monasteries, and their lands and possessions were confiscated. In the Gaelic areas there was little enthusiasm for these changes, and in the places that were most removed from

Pl. 74—Murrisk Abbey.

THE ABBEY OF MURRISK

Murrisk Abbey at the bottom of Croagh Patrick is celebrated in an eighteenth-century song 'The Abbey of Murrisk' recorded by the folksong collector Edward Bunting:

> *Céud slán don teach úd ann a mbin uair*
> *Ar mo thráthuibh mhór fhada láimh leis a cruaich*
> *Bheadh na ceólta bin ó fhlaithios gabháil chuguin a mias*
> *Agas na sléibhte cur meala ó dheas 's ó thuaigh.*

> A thousand farewells to the Abbey where they read
> The long matins and hours by the side of the Cruach,
> Where the sweetest music sounds from heaven coming down,
> And mountains yield honey from the North and South.

Pl. 75—Carved head at Murrisk Abbey.

There are several carved human heads at Murrisk Abbey, including this bearded figure smiling mischievously at visitors.

Pl. 76—Detail of a wall painting at Clare Island Abbey.

WALL PAINTINGS

Today these medieval abbeys and churches appear grey and dull buildings. However, during their use in the medieval period they were generally whitewashed externally and sometimes quite colourful internally, with painted frescoes decorating the walls and ceilings. Such paintings rarely survive the damp Irish climate; however, portions have miraculously survived at Clare Island. These wall paintings have recently been restored and are among the best-preserved in the country. They occur on the walls and the vaulted ceiling of the chancel. Among the scenes depicted is a cattle raid, reflecting a custom of the Gaelic chieftains such as the O'Malleys. A curiosity among the paintings is this dragon.

English rule in Dublin, such as West Mayo, they did not take effect for several decades. In fact the friars at both Burrishoole Abbey and Murrisk Abbey continued to live there well into the eighteenth century.

GRACE O'MALLEY (GRANUAILE) AND THE ENGLISH CONQUEST

In the long run, and particularly under the rule of Queen Elizabeth, the Tudor English were able to take advantage of the disunity that typified the Gaelic clans, and they gradually gained total control of the country. Gráinne, or Grace, O'Malley, alias Granuaile, became the best known of the seafaring O'Malley family and came to symbolise the final stand of the Gaelic Irish in West Mayo against the English monarchy.

Granuaile, daughter of Dubhdara ('Black Oak') O'Malley, was born in 1530, according to tradition at Belclare Castle, which stood near Westport. At the age of fifteen she married Dónal O'Flaherty (alias Dónal an Chogaidh, 'Dónal of the Battles'), who was a chieftain of Connemara and an ally of the O'Malleys in war. From the O'Flaherty castle at Bunowen on the west coast of Connemara, Grace took to looting ships bound for the town of Galway. Following the murder of her husband Dónal by the Joyce clan of the Lough Corrib area, Grace returned to West Mayo with at least three galleys. In 1566 she married Richard an Iarainn Burke, who owned Carrigahowley, or Rockfleet Castle. So renowned a character was his wife that Richard subsequently became known as the husband of Granuaile.

Shortly afterwards Granuaile gave birth to a son, Tiobóid na Long, 'Toby of the Ships'. Legend has it that he was born at sea and that the next day Granuaile led her fleet into battle with Algerian pirates. According to the practice of the day, Tiobóid was fostered as a boy by Edmund MacTibbot at Castleaffy. This was one way in which a powerful family maintained the loyalty of its followers. In a poem composed in his honour he was celebrated as

Tiobóid Burke of the valiant feats
Of the hawklike blue eye...
He is the warrior whose curving neck
With ringleted golden-yellow hair
Is secretly loved by girls in every region
He is the ruddy-cheeked heir of Gráinne.

In 1576 Sir Henry Sidney, lord deputy of Ireland, wrote from Galway that 'there came to mee also a most famous femynyne sea capten called Grany Imallye [Gráinne O'Malley], and offered her service unto me, wheresoever I woulde command her, with three gallyes and two hundred fightinge men...This was a notorious woman in all the coast of Ireland.' In so doing Granuaile hoped to illustrate her power so that Sidney would see her as an ally rather than an

CLARE ISLAND TOWER-HOUSE

This tower-house on Clare Island was probably built by the O'Malleys at the beginning of the fifteenth century. Today it overlooks the island harbour, and during the fifteenth and sixteenth centuries the widely renowned and feared fleets of the O'Malleys probably moored here. According to tradition, Grace O'Malley lived here for a time, and Caesar Otway, writing his *Tour of Connaught* in 1838, recorded a rather fanciful story that 'in her castle at Clare Island, where her swiftest vessels were stationed, the cable of her chief galley was passed through a hole made for that purpose in the wall and fastened to her bed-post, in order that she might be the more readily alarmed in case of an attempted surprise'.

Pl. 77—Clare Island tower-house.

enemy. However, only weeks later Granuaile went on a mission to plunder the earl of Desmond of Munster, only to be captured by the earl and imprisoned in Askeaton Castle and then Limerick Gaol for a year and a half. Lord Justice Drury, who was delighted at her capture, described her as 'a woman that hath impudently passed the part of womanhood and been a great spoiler and chief commander and director of thieves and murderers at sea'. In November 1578 Grace was transferred to Dublin Castle, and by March of the following year she was, for some unknown reason, released. Immediately on her arrival home to Rockfleet Castle she was besieged by a garrison of soldiers sent by the sheriff of Galway in reprisal for attacks on Galway shipping. Granuaile successfully repulsed the attack commanded by Captain Martin, who narrowly escaped being made prisoner.

Later, in 1579, the Burkes answered the call to a rebellion by the earl of Desmond in Munster. The Burkes, O'Malleys and O'Flahertys marched into Galway. In February 1580 Sir Nicholas Malby, the English governor of Connacht, returned from Munster to face the rebellion of the Burkes. Richard Burke retreated to Clew Bay and was followed there by Malby. Malby met Grace O'Malley at Ballyknock Castle and later went to Burrishoole Abbey, which he had fortified and garrisoned. Soon afterwards Richard Burke submitted, but with little consequence despite his rebellion, as Malby was forced to return to Munster, where there was further unrest.

Granuaile's husband, Richard Burke, belonged to a senior branch of the Burke family. The most senior title within the Burke chieftains of Mayo was the MacWilliam. In 1571 Shane MacOliverus Burke was elected MacWilliam, and Richard Burke was elected his *tánaiste* ('successor'). In November 1580 the MacWilliam died, and under Gaelic law the title should have been passed onto Richard Burke. However, under English law the title went to the next of kin of Shane Burke. Granuaile combined forces with Richard to fight for his right to the MacWilliamship, mustering a huge army of nearly 2500 soldiers, many of them mercenary gallowglasses. Sir Nicholas Malby marched into Mayo and met Richard. Following negotiations a deal was struck, and Richard was granted a knighthood and allowed to retain the MacWilliam title in return for obeying English rule and the Queen's representative. Richard also agreed to pay a rent of 50 cows or 250 marks each year and to provide food and lodging for 200 soldiers for up to 42 days each year. This was a small price to pay, for with the title he acquired extensive territories in south Mayo. He moved with Granuaile to a large castle on the eastern shores of Lough Mask. In October 1582 Malby held a gathering in Galway of the Connacht chieftains. He wrote of his guests: 'among them Grany O'Malley is one and thinketh herself to be no small lady'.

However, Richard and Granuaile did not enjoy their new-found wealth for very long. On 30 April 1583 Richard died. His death is recorded in the Annals of the Four Masters, where he is described as 'a plundering, warlike, unquiet and rebellious man, who had often forced the gap of danger upon his enemies and upon whom it was frequently forced'. Grace returned to her husband's castle at Rockfleet on the shores of Clew Bay. Sir Nicholas Malby died the following year, and Sir Richard Bingham succeeded him as governor of Connacht. Bingham believed that the 'Irish were never tamed with words but with swords' and claimed that Granuaile was a 'nurse to all rebellions in the province for forty years'. His approach to dealing with Gaelic chieftains such as Granuaile and many of her relations was very different from his predecessor's. The issue of the MacWilliam title was always a contentious one, and in 1585 the Burkes were in rebellion against Bingham over claims to the title. Among them was Granuaile's son Tiobóid Burke and Richard Burke (alias 'The Devil's

ROCKFLEET TOWER-HOUSE

'The Spanish Captain, sailing by
For Newport, with amazement
Beheld the cannon'd longship lie
Moor'd to the lady's casement;
And, covering coin and cup of gold
In haste their hatches under,
They whispered 'Tis a pirate's hold;
She sails the seas for plunder'.
(extract from a song entitled 'Grace O'Malley' by Sir
Samuel Ferguson)

This tower-house was the residence of the Burkes and was for a time the home of Grace O'Malley after the death of her second husband, Richard Burke. In their tour of 1842 Mr and Mrs Hall considered that 'the whole character of the building [was] that of savage strength'. They were told 'that the castle is supposed to contain a hoard of wealth beneath its vaults, which is scrupulously guarded from sunset to sunrise by a mounted horseman, who perambulates the verge of the buildings, and effectually keeps off all intruders'.

Pls 78 and 79—Rockfleet tower-house.

Hook'), who was married to her daughter Margaret from her first marriage to Dónal O'Flaherty.

The tension eased for a short time, and in 1587 Grace went to Dublin, where she and her sons received a pardon for past offences from Queen Elizabeth. However, in September 1588 a new threat to the English government arrived in Ireland in the form of the Spanish Armada, which was wrecked in terrible storms off the west coast of Ireland. It is believed that five Armada ships were wrecked off the Mayo coast, including the 1160-ton *El Gran Grin,* carrying 329 men and 28 guns, which struck rocks off Clare Island. About 200 of the *El Gran Grin* crew drowned, with the remainder, including the commander, Don Pedro de Mendoza, surviving. It is believed that Mendoza and over sixty others were later killed in an attempt to escape their O'Malley hosts; however, the O'Malleys and Burkes were accused of harbouring the Spaniards, which was considered treasonable. In 1589 Bingham ordered the sheriff of Mayo, John Browne (descendant of the Brownes of Westport House), to enter Burrishoole with an army of 250 soldiers. Shortly after stopping at Rockfleet Castle he continued west beyond Mulranny, where he was attacked and killed by 'The Devil's Hook', Granuaile's son-in-law. Later Bingham himself came to Mayo with an army of 1000; he plundered the area, and Granuaile and her followers were forced to take refuge on the islands of Clew Bay. By 1592 her son Tióbóid and her stepson Edmund Burke were the only two chieftains in West Mayo not to have submitted to Bingham's army. However, Bingham ordered a fleet of ships to attack the islands that the O'Malleys and Burkes had for so long used as places of refuge. By September of that year Tióbóid had submitted to Bingham at Aghagower.

Granuaile now felt persecuted by Bingham's soldiers, and in 1593 she made the daring journey to England, where she was granted an audience with Queen Elizabeth. While she was away, Bingham feared that she might succeed in undermining his authority in Connacht, so he had her son Tióbóid imprisoned at Athlone on the charge of treason, a crime punishable by death. He also imprisoned her half-brother Dónal na Piopa ('Donal the Piper') O'Malley and charged him with the murder of a number of soldiers. Grace's petition to the Queen was endorsed by the earl of Ormond, who had a claim to the lands owned by the Butlers of the thirteenth century in Burrishoole, where Granuaile lived. Her petition played on the fact that she was a widow with no dowry, and she asked 'in tender considercion whereof and in regard of her great age...to grant her some reasonable maintenance for the little tyme she hath to lyve'. In return for her protection and maintenance, Grace promised to surrender her lands and military support to the Queen.

Queen Elizabeth was obviously highly impressed by the Irish chieftain: she granted Granuaile a pardon and ordered the release of her son Tióbóid na Long and half-brother Dónal na Piopa. Furthermore, she implored Bingham to 'protect them to live in peace to enjoy their livelihoods', further commenting that Granuaile had 'departeth with great thankfulness and with many earnest

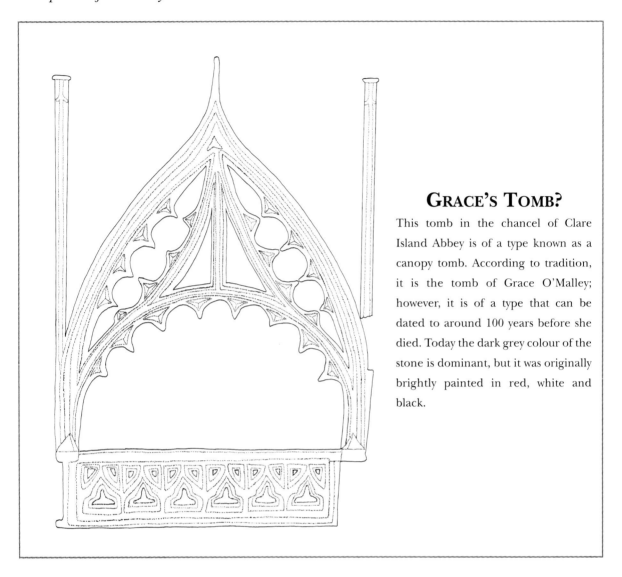

GRACE'S TOMB?

This tomb in the chancel of Clare Island Abbey is of a type known as a canopy tomb. According to tradition, it is the tomb of Grace O'Malley; however, it is of a type that can be dated to around 100 years before she died. Today the dark grey colour of the stone is dominant, but it was originally brightly painted in red, white and black.

Fig. 16—Clare Island canopy tomb.

promises that she will, as long as she lives, continue a dutiful subject'.

The final years of the sixteenth century saw considerable unrest, with several rebellions against the Crown by Gaelic chieftains, especially those in Ulster. These rebellions frequently spilled over into the rest of the country. In 1595 Red Hugh O'Donnell, leader of a confederacy of Ulster chieftains against the English, put forward his own candidate for the title of MacWilliam, Theobald Burke from north Mayo. However, Theobald failed to gain the support of the other Mayo Burkes. O'Donnell's action alienated the Mayo Burkes, and he was unable to persuade them fully to support his rebellion against the Crown. O'Donnell made several attempts to force their allegiance, and in 1599 he sent Niall Garv O'Donnell into west Connacht, who attacked the MacGibbons at their crannog on Lough Lahardaun near Aghagower. In the battle eighteen men of the MacGibbons were slaughtered.

During this unrest Granuaile and her son Tiobóid Burke were pressured to take sides, but Tiobóid soon realised the worth of continued loyalty to the Crown. As late as 1599 it was reported to the new English governor of Connacht, Sir Conyers Clifford, that 'the O'Malleys are much feared everywhere by sea'. Furthermore, he was told that the O'Malley galleys were capable of carrying 300 men apiece and that they would be very useful for the Queen's campaign in Ulster. Clearly the Crown also saw the value of the loyalty of Tiobóid Burke and his O'Malley relatives. Tiobóid did not immediately reap the rewards of his loyalty, but eventually he regained much of the land previously acquired by his father in the short period for which he had held the MacWilliam title. The MacWilliam title itself was not officially revived; however, in 1627 Tiobóid was by way of compensation given the new title Viscount Mayo.

Little is known of the final years of Grace O'Malley. Legend has it that she died in 1603 at Rockfleet and was buried in the Cistercian Abbey on Clare Island. Throughout her life she had maintained her maiden name and an independent reputation in a violent, male-oriented society. The English governor of Connacht, Sir Richard Bingham, had commented on 'her naughty disposicion towards the state'; however, there was no sense of a unified or nationalist identity at this time. The period was one of almost-constant upheaval, with internal feuding and rebellion. After the death of her husband Richard Burke, Grace fought to maintain her independence and that of her family. Her success is testified to by the rise of her son Tiobóid na Long as the most powerful landowner in Mayo.

The modern era

The collapse of the Gaelic way of life and the consolidation of English rule throughout the country was finalised in 1600 at the Battle of Kinsale in County Cork, during which Tiobóid na Long (Granuaile's son) fought on the side of the English Crown, with 160 men. The following years saw the flight of many Gaelic lords from Ireland, a tragic event that became known as the Flight of the Earls, or Wild Geese. A ballad by Thomas Lavelle captures the sadness of banishment:

> When I dwelt at home in plenty, and my gold did much abound,
> In company of fair young maids the Spanish ale went round.
> Tis bitter change from those gay days, and now I am forced to go,
> And must leave my bones in Santa Cruz, far from my own Mayo.

Two families that remained in Mayo were the Burkes and the O'Malleys. The marriage of Grace O'Malley to Richard Burke symbolised the allegiance between these two families at the end of the sixteenth century, and their son Tiobóid na Long became the greatest landowner in the county. This was an unusual position for any Gaelic chieftain at the beginning of the seventeenth century, particularly one who had a history of revolt against the English

Pl. 80— Viscount Mayo Chalice.

VISCOUNT MAYO CHALICE

This silver chalice was donated to the friars of Murrisk Abbey in 1635, although the abbey had been officially dissolved a century earlier. Around the base of the chalice is the inscription 'Pray for the souls of Theobald Lord Viscount Mayo and his wife Maeve O'Conor who had me made for the monastery of Murrisk in the year of the Lord 1635'. Theobald Lord Viscount Mayo is probably Tiobóid na Long Burke, son of Grace O'Malley, although he had died six years before the chalice was donated.

CROMWELLIAN PERIOD

In the middle of the seventeenth century came renewed conflict when the English Civil War raged in Ireland, and Cromwellian troops took over and refortified Burrishoole Abbey in 1653. According to tradition, the troops stripped naked two nuns, Sister Honoria Magaen and Sister Honoria Burke, both over 100 years of age. The two nuns were then thrown into a boat on Lake Furnace and left on Saint's Island, where they died of their injuries. Sister Honoria Burke was the daughter of Richard an Iarainn Burke, the second husband of Grace O'Malley, and the stepsister of their son Tióbóid na Long.

Pl. 81—Burrishoole Abbey.

Fig. 17—Detail of inscription on O'Kelly tomb, Burrishoole Abbey.

At the beginning of the seventeenth century the O'Kelly family came to Burrishoole, and they were prominent in the area for a time. During the Cromwellian period some years later, their lands were confiscated. In the south transept of Burrishoole Abbey is an altar tomb with a Latin inscription featuring some curious decorative details. The inscription reads:

Orate pro anima Davidis oge Kelly, qui me fieri fecit, sibi heredibus suis, Anno Domini 1623, et ejus uxori Anabla Barrett.

Pray for the soul of David Kelly junior, who caused me to be made, for himself and his heirs A.D. 1623, and (for the soul) of his wife Annabel Barrett.

administration and its monarchy. The outcome of his acceptance of English rule was that in 1603 Tióbóid received a knighthood from James I, and in 1627 he was appointed first Viscount Mayo by Charles I. Tióbóid died two years later and was buried at Ballintubber Abbey.

By the middle of the seventeenth century many old Gaelic families that had remained in Ireland had been dispossessed of their lands and transplanted to Connacht by Cromwell's administration. The third Viscount Mayo, Theobald Burke (grandson of Tióbóid na Long) was executed in Galway by the Cromwellians, and the family estate was confiscated. With the restoration of King Charles II some years later, the lands returned to the fourth Viscount Mayo, another Theobald Burke. However, the lands of the estate came into the hands of the Browne family through the marriage in 1669 of Maud Burke (sister of the fourth Viscount Mayo) to Colonel John Browne, a barrister. Browne inherited the castle known as Cathair na Mart, which was later incorporated into the present-day Westport House. John Browne, a Jacobite, was a personal friend of Patrick Sarsfield. Browne used his ironworks at Knappagh to produce bayonets, shot and cannonballs for two regiments of soldiers he had enlisted. Browne and his two regiments fought with Sarsfield in

Pl. 82—Plaque at Murrisk Abbey.

MURRISK PLAQUE

A stone plaque at Murrisk Abbey has the O'Malley coat of arms, together with the three lions of the Browne family crest. The stone is dated to 1719, the year Martha Browne of Neale died, and it was probably commissioned to commemorate her marriage in 1675 to Captain Owen Mór O'Malley of Burrishoole. The Burkes had lost their dominance in West Mayo during the seventeenth century and were replaced by the Brownes. However, the O'Malleys continued as important landowners throughout this period, until the present day.

1691 on the side of King James II at Limerick, which was besieged by the armies of William of Orange. Colonel Maney O'Donel of Newport also fought on the Jacobean side at Limerick. The downfall of James II and the rise of William of Orange saw the final transfer of land from Catholics to Protestants.

THE PENAL ERA

Following the victory of William of Orange, Penal Laws were enforced and the Catholic church was suppressed. Particularly in rural areas, no new Catholic churches were built, and instead local people attended open-air services at

Pls 83 and 84— Srahwee wedge tomb.

The wedge tomb at Srahwee is locally called *Altóir* from its use as an altar for outdoor Catholic masses during the Penal times of the eighteenth century, and there is a small cross carved onto the roof stone. The tomb is sheltered by a knoll of rock, from which a lookout could be kept for the authorities, who had outlawed priests. The tomb overlooks Lough Nahaltora ('lake of the the altar'), and beside it is a dried-up holy well.

*Pl. 85—
Kilgeever
holy well.*

KILGEEVER HOLY WELL

The holy well at Kilgeever is known locally as *Tober Rigan Domnaig*, 'Our Lord's well of the Sabbath'. Traditionally, pilgrims came in large numbers to the well on 15 July, and many come as part of their pilgrimage to Croagh Patrick on the last Sunday of July. Caesar Otway during his 1838 tour of Connacht met Revd Charles Seymour, who had been perpetual curate at Louisburgh some years earlier. Seymour was a Calvinist and scathing of native Catholic traditions, although he was fluent in Irish. When Otway met Seymour he was in his retirement; however, despite Catholic Emancipation some years earlier, he was still very critical of what he saw as uneducated, peasant Catholics in constant need of reproach. Otway recalled an incident during an outing when Seymour stopped a man who was apparently an invalid:

' "Where are you going, my poor fellow?" "Och, then your honour, where would I be going but to the holy well of Kilgeever, and from far and away I have come, blessed be God, Patrick, and all the saints, for I am tould and believe that if I am washed in the blessed well, I will get strength not only to stand, but also to do my stations at the Reek". Assuming at once an air of authority, S[eymour] cried out to a man dressed in the uniform of the coast-guard: "Come here, sir, and take this man into custody; I know him to be an impostor; he can walk as well as you or I, and he *shall* walk without help of barrow or crutch to the Bridewell [prison] of Westport". The fellow was taken by surprise, he supposed he was in the presence of a magistrate, who by some means had got information of his roguery, and he actually bounced up, started off from his go-cart, and made for the face of the hill, with the activity of a mountain sheep. This was exactly what S[eymour] wanted; he immediately addressed the people in Irish—showed how *he* could perform a miracle more satisfactory than the holy well…"Boys, would it not save your faith very much from being abused, if I were always here to try my hand on every cripple, before he washed in the holy well of Kilgeever?".'

specially built altars, frequently located at the many ancient church ruins that were scattered throughout the countryside. At Lankill is a Penal altar where Sean na Sagart, who had been hired by the authorities to spy on priests, claimed that he had seen 28 priests being ordained by the Revd Owen O'Duffy. 'St Patrick's Chair' at Boheh, covered in rock art dating to the Neolithic period several thousand years before, may also have been used as a Penal altar. Near the graveyard at Boheh a cairn of stones known locally as the Priests' Grave allegedly marks the grave of two priests, possibly killed during Penal times. Catholic children were not allowed a formal education, and in the absence of official schools 'hedge schools' were commonly used in the countryside, where a local teacher gave outdoor lessons to pupils. One such hedge school was located beneath some bushes in the corner of a field at Tully near Louisburgh. The teacher, who lived in a tiny cottage nearby, earned the name 'Horse' Moran because he ploughed his plot of land himself, without the aid of a horse.

WESTPORT AND THE BROWNE FAMILY

After the defeat of James II by William of Orange, Colonel John Browne seems to have abandoned Westport House and built a house near Aghagower known as Mount Browne. He was succeeded by his eldest son, Peter Browne, who also inherited his father's debts, incurred by his participation in the Siege of Limerick. There is a stone with the inscription 'Pray for the soul of Peter Browne who caused me to be made 1723' in a ringfort at Carrownalurgan near Westport. This probably came from an altar commissioned by Browne, and it is believed that it belonged to a Penal church that was merely a barn. However, it seems more likely that the altar stone originally came from the nearby church at Oughaval, which may have fallen into disuse after Peter Browne's death and was replaced soon afterwards by the Protestant church in the grounds of Westport House. Peter Browne died in 1724 and was buried at Burrishoole Abbey. That same year he had presented a chalice to the friars of Murrisk.

Peter Browne's daughters were Catholics, but his son, John Denis Browne, was converted to Protestantism in order that he could inherit the Westport estate; according to the Penal Laws, a Catholic could not inherit land. John Denis was orphaned at the age of fifteen and was sent by his guardian to Oxford for education. On his return to Westport in 1729 John Denis inherited the estate and married Anne Gore, sister of the earl of Arran. He was the first to receive the title earl of Altamont. In 1732 he had Westport House rebuilt to the design of Richard Cassels, who was a little-known architect at the time but later designed some of the most prestigious houses in Ireland. John Denis continued to live at Mount Browne while Westport House was rebuilt. In 1734 the house bridge was constructed and in 1736 the two waterfalls and church in the grounds were built.

The original village of Westport clustered around Westport House and the nearby church. However, as can be seen in a painting of 1760 by George Moore,

*Fig. 18—
Painting of
Westport
House by
George
Moore, 1760
(courtesy of
the marquess
of Sligo ©).*

WESTPORT HOUSE

Work began on Westport House in 1680 by Colonel John Browne near the site of an earlier castle known as *Cathair na Mart*. In 1734 his grandson, John Denis Browne, first earl of Altamont, commissioned Richard Cassels to redesign the house. The east front of the present house is the best example of his work remaining: a nine-bay façade with winged eagles at either end of the cornice, which are part of the family crest. The church, now in ruins, in the grounds of the house was built in 1736. In 1752 Dr Pococke visited John Browne at Westport House and wrote: 'Mr Browne's house is very pleasantly situated on the South side of the rivlet over which he has built two handsome bridges, & has form'd Cascades in the river which are seen from the front of the house...It is an exceeding good house & well finished, the design & execution of Mr Castels: Mr Brown designs to remove the Village & make it a Park Improvement all round; there are fine low hills every way which are planted & improved, & the trees grown exceedingly well: the tyde comes just up to the house; & the Cascades are fine salmon leaps.' Sometime after 1760, the year this painting by George Moore was done, Browne had completed his redesign of the gardens and parkland and had moved the town of Westport to its present location. George Moore lived at Moore Hall on the shores of Lough Carra and had married Louisa Browne, a cousin of John Denis Browne.

the village had been cleared to make way for the gardens and moved to where the town now stands. The building of modern-day Westport began in around 1760. On 17 March of that year a notice appeared in the *Dublin Journal* inviting tenders for the construction of the new town, to the design of the little-known architect William Leeson, who seems to have been aided by Lord Altamont's eldest son, Peter Browne. Construction probably began soon afterwards, and the development of the town was heightened in the early 1770s with the introduction of the linen industry. Houses were built by Lord Altamont for weavers, who were given an incentive of low, long-term leases. The industry grew from almost nothing in 1772 to sales of £10,000 in 1776. The English traveller and agriculturist Arthur Young visited Westport and noted the industrious and progressive endeavours of Browne:

> In Lord Altamont I found an improver whose works deserved the closest attention; he very readily favoured me with the following account: He began to improve mountain land in 1768, and has every year since done some, making it a rule to employ whatever labourers offer for work...In introducing the linen manufacture, his Lordship has made great exertions...In order to establish it, he built good houses in the town of Westport, and let them upon very reasonable terms to weavers, gave them looms and lent them money to buy yarn...This year he has also given such encouragement as to induce a person to build and establish a bleach green and mill. The progress of this manufacture has been prodigious.

In 1776 the second earl of Altamont, Peter Browne, inherited his father's estate. Some years earlier he had married Elizabeth Kelly, the heiress to great sugar plantations in Jamaica, and the family became one of the richest in the country. He held the title until his death in 1780, when he was succeeded by his son, John Denis Browne, the third earl of Altamont. With his inherited fortune the earl could afford to expand the town and create a port. By the end of the 1780s he had the streets of Westport laid out as they survive today, and the Octagon and Market House became the focus of the town. Local farmers processed flax, which was then sold as yarn to weavers in the Market House. The weavers turned the yarn into webs of coarse linen cloth for sale to the agents of the local and northern merchants. Much of the linen was shipped from the quays at Westport to northern Ireland and Glasgow in Scotland. Two oatmills, a flourmill, a brewery and a threshing mill were also established in the town at this time.

In 1795 large numbers of families migrated from the north of Ireland to Westport, bringing many new trades and skills to the town and the surrounding countryside. In this year the village of Louisburgh was founded by the third earl of Altamont, John Denis Browne. The town was named after Louisburgh in Nova Scotia, where his uncle Henry had fought on the British side in a battle against the French in 1758. Also, an uncle of Louisa Catherine Howe, the wife

BURRISHOOLE ABBEY

In Grose's *Antiquities of Ireland* (1796) is an engraved drawing of Burrishoole Abbey copied in 1793 from an original painting by the Italian antiquarian artist Angelo Bigari, who had accompanied another antiquarian painter, Gabriel Beranger, on a tour of Connacht. The tour was documented by Beranger, and on 17 July 1779 the two painters made drawings and plans of Burrishoole Abbey. Beranger recalled: 'We were surrounded by a vast number of people, amongst whom we observed some uncommon whisperings, and goings and comings. Mr. Bigari thought that their intention was to rob us; but we came off safe, and returned to Newport.' Two days later Beranger and Bigari dined at Westport House with Lord Altamont, who told them that they 'were near being seized by the people of Burryshool, who had taken us for spies; that they had applied to him for an order to lodge us in jail, but that he had charged them at their peril not to molest us, as he knew our business—which accounted for their uncommon behaviour whilst we were amongst them.'

Fig. 19—Engraving of Burrishoole Abbey.

of the third earl, had commanded a regiment at this battle.

At the beginning of the eighteenth century an important western port was established at Newport by Captain Pratt, and for many years the town was known as Newport-Pratt. Some years later James Moore, the land agent of the absentee landlords the Medlycotts, supervised the building of the quays at Newport, and the town continued to thrive. By the end of the eighteenth century the

CROAGH PATRICK

Gabriel Beranger, who painted this watercolour of Croagh Patrick in 1779, wrote that 'the summit, in the form of a cone, is generally enveloped by clouds; and though it appears pointy, has a large area at its top, where there is a stone altar built, on which mass is said on the saint's day. I believe it to have been formerly a volcano—at least it has very much the look of one'. During his stay in Westport, Beranger was received and entertained by Lord Altamont at Westport House. He later wrote: 'After diner, his Lordship showed us his wolf-dogs, three in number; they are amazing large, white, with black spots, but of the make and shape of the greyhound, only the head and neck somewhat larger in proportion.' It seems that these wolfhounds were the last of the original breed known in Ireland. The year after Beranger saw them, one of the wolfhounds, called Prime Serjeant, was shot by 'Fighting' (George Robert) Fitzgerald, from Turlough near Castlebar, in anger with Denis Browne, high sheriff and brother of the third earl of Altamont. Fitzgerald shot the dog on the pretext that it was a menace, and Browne was obliged to issue a challenge to a duel. When they met they chose broadswords as their weapons; however, Fitzgerald without warning fired a pistol at Browne, barely missing him. Browne refused to proceed with the duel and initiated legal proceedings that proved unsuccessful. Later, Denis Browne, also known as 'Denis the Rope', had Fitzgerald hanged for a separate offence.

Fig. 20—Watercolour of Croagh Patrick by Gabriel Beranger (courtesy of the Royal Irish Academy ©).

O'Donels were the dominant landowners in the area, having acquired much of the Medlycott estate and built Newport House. Sir Neal O'Donel was the driving force behind the rise of the O'Donels; he owned his own ship, and his income was supplemented by smuggling. In 1790 revenue officials seized several casks of wine at his house at Milcum (a corruption of the name Melcomb in Dorsetshire, from where the previous owners, the Binghams, came). Sir Neal sued the Crown for trespass and forceful entry and was awarded damages of £1500.

McParlan's 1801 *Statistical survey of County Mayo* recorded that in Newport 'every cabin has a loom. They spin and weave pieces of linen for the Castlebar and Westport markets...There are now in Newport upwards of a hundred girls employed in a straw hat manufactory...People wear the hats, not for charity, but for their fineness and excellence.'

1798 REBELLION

The French Revolution inspired in this country the founding of the United Irishmen, and a Mayo branch was formed by John Gibbons, an agent of Lord Altamont. In August 1798 the United Irishmen instigated a rebellion, aided by French troops under the command of General Humbert, who landed at Killala in north Mayo. James McDonnell, general of the Irish forces, took over Westport House as headquarters of the West Mayo rebels. Other local rebel leaders were Fr Myles Prendergast of Murrisk and Fr Manus Sweeney of Newport. The rebellion was finally defeated by British troops at the Battle of Ballinamuck in County Longford. Sir Neal O'Donel's son, Neal Beg, fought on the British side at Ballinamuck as captain in the Louth militia. John Gibbons of Westport fled to France; however, his son, also John, was hanged for his part in the revolution by his godfather, Denis Browne, brother of the third earl of Altamont and high sheriff of Mayo. At Lankill is a bridge that was known as 'Hangman's Bridge', because tradition holds that rebels were hanged here after returning from the Battle of Ballinamuck. For his part in the rebellion Fr Manus Sweeney was hanged, allegedly from the market crane in Newport, and was buried at Burrishoole Abbey. Today the original flag of the Mayo Legion is on display at Westport House. The flag was made especially by the women of France and was brought by General Humbert on his landing at Killala in 1798.

The 1798 Rebellion prompted a debate in the Irish parliament on an Act of Union with the United Kingdom, which would effectively disband the Irish parliament and mean that Ireland was directly ruled by the British houses of parliament in London. During a parliamentary debate on the Union in 1799 Colonel Hugh O'Donel, eldest son of Sir Neal O'Donel of Newport, stated: 'There is no person in or out of this House who can be more anxious for supporting the closest connection between England and Ireland than I have been or ever shall. I have fought to preserve it from being interrupted by external and internal foes; but should the legislative independence of Ireland be voted away by a Parliament which is not competent therewith I shall hold myself discharged of my allegiance and I will join the people in rich clothes as I have ever done the rebels in rags. If my opposition to it in this House shall not be successful I will oppose it in the field.' His was an unusually strong stance against the *proposed* Union, despite having been offered a substantial sum of money and the title earl of Achill, but Colonel O'Donel died in October of that year and did not live long enough to act on his fighting words.

NINETEENTH-CENTURY WESTPORT

The Act of Union was passed in 1800 and was supported by the third earl of Altamont, who had been offered and now received the new title marquess of Sligo. During the years following the Act of Union Westport continued to expand and developed into a fine Georgian town. The Carrowbeg River was canalised and lined with trees, forming a riverside boulevard. By 1818 Westport Quay was a fully developed port, with custom house, storehouses and a lighthouse, and replaced Newport as the primary port of Clew Bay. At the invitation of George Clendinning, agent to the first marquess of Sligo, the Bank of Ireland established one of its first branches outside Dublin in Westport in 1825. The Railway Hotel was then known as Robinsons and had been built and furnished by the first marquess of Sligo. Many nineteenth-century travel writers stayed there, and one, William Thackeray, in 1842 described it as 'one of the prettiest, comfortablest inns in Ireland'.

The second marquess of Sligo, Howe Peter Browne, was a colourful character, and among his friends were George IV (godfather to his eldest son) and Lord Byron. While on a grand tour of the Mediterranean the second marquess was impressed by the similarity of Delphi to his fisheries at Doo Lough, after which he named the area Delphi. While in Greece, he excavated at Mycenae and found large columns belonging to the Treasury of Atreus. He decided to take these back to Westport, and to ensure their safe passage he bribed two British seamen. This was a serious offence for which in 1812 he received a fine of £5000 and was sentenced to four months in Newgate prison. Bizarrely, his widowed mother married the judge in his trial. In 1906 the sixth marquess presented the Greek columns to the British Museum, and replicas of the columns were used in the south wing of Westport House.

On his release from prison the second marquess commissioned a racecourse at Ballyknock, outside Westport. He was fond of horseracing, having won many trophies, and in 1811 his horse Waxy had won the English Derby. In 1812 he won a wager of 1000 guineas by driving a coach from London to Holyhead (270 miles) in 35 hours. There was also a responsible side to the second marquess, who in 1834 as governor of Jamaica abolished slavery, thereby losing large revenues from his Jamaican estates. This gesture paralleled the efforts of Daniel O'Connell in Ireland, who had successfully overturned the Penal Laws, thereby achieving emancipation for Catholics.

WESTPORT PORT

During the early 1780s Westport Harbour was provided with a quayfront and warehouses. On one of the warehouses is a stone with the date 1783 and the initials of Charles McDonnell, one of the merchants encouraged to set up in Westport by Lord Altamont. Textiles and agricultural produce were the main exports. During the early 1800s the port continued to expand, and the channel was deepened to admit ships of 200 tons in burden to moor. Additional warehouses six or seven storeys high and a custom house were built. However, by the time this engraving by W.H. Bartlett was published the economy of Westport was in decline. Indeed, this portrayal of a busy port may be largely the result of artistic licence, and William Thackeray, who visited the port only three years later (1842), was perhaps harshly dismissive: 'As for the warehouses, they are enormous; and might accommodate, I should think, not only the trade of Westport, but of Manchester too...These dismal mausoleums, as vast as pyramids, are the place where the dead trade of Westport lies buried—a trade that, in its lifetime, probably was about as big as a mouse.'

Fig. 21—Westport port by W.H. Bartlett, c. 1839, reproduced in Scenery and Antiquities of Ireland.

O'Connell now turned his energies towards repealing the Act of Union with Great Britain, so that Ireland might rule itself as an independent kingdom. In 1843 O'Connell spoke at several large meetings around Mayo, and the Repeal Movement gained momentum. His right-hand man, Robert Dillon Browne, visited Westport in August 1843. On his approach to the town, he was greeted by two Repeal flags that had been erected on the Bronze Age burial mound at Sheean. *The Telegraph* reported on the events:

Westport—the Tory capital of Murrisk, and the very focus of Mayo Orangism—has come out unmistakeably on the repeal question. TWENTY THOUSAND of the inhabitants of that and the surrounding districts, including the patriotic and ever-faithful parish of Kilmeena, Aughagower, Louisburgh, Murrisk, Newport, Burrishoole, and Ross, headed by their respective pastors, assembled on Thursday last at the Fair-green to declare their unalterable resolve never to cease agitating until the odious and iniquitous act of Union is altogether wiped off the face of the English statute book.

The paper's correspondent also reported that Browne declared in his speech that.

Everything around him proclaimed that she [Ireland] should be a nation. The very voice of the billows that laved the base of Croaghpatrick murmured out sweet sounds that Ireland should not continue any longer a degraded province. That voice was borne to the mountain's top, and carried off on the receding tide until it was echoed back again from the land of liberty and Washington (loud and continued cheering).

This air of optimism was also evident at the agricultural show held in September of 1843 by the Westport and Newport Agricultural Improvement Society, which had been founded less than a year earlier. The show was held in the farmyard of Westport House, and a journalist for *The Telegraph* reported that Sir Richard O'Donel's 'mangel-wurzel [a variety of beet] deservedly bore away the palm: but Mr. Garvey was awarded first prize for turnips and carrots. One of the turnips (*Aberdeen*) weighed 22lbs, and several of the Swedish description averaged 18lbs each'. Sir Richard O'Donel also had four Swiss cows and bulls at the show. Later that evening two hundred people had dinner at the courthouse. Food and fine wines were plentiful that night; however, this show of agricultural successes could do little to prevent the catastrophe about to hit the small Mayo farmers.

THE FAMINE

The economic boom soon began to weaken, and from the end of the Napoleonic Wars in 1815 the demand from Britain for textiles and food declined. The economy of Westport was unable to compete with the industrialised power-spinning established in the north of Ireland. Gradual economic decline followed, and poverty became increasingly common, so much so that in autumn 1835 the English traveller John Barrow reported that on his way to the Reek 'we passed some of the most miserable hovels that I have yet seen...so bad that without being convinced myself of the fact, I should scarcely have supposed them to be habitations of human beings, but rather as sheds for the cattle'. In 1841 the foundation stone was laid for a workhouse in Westport, to house and feed the destitute, with a capacity for 5000 inmates. In his *Irish sketch-book* (1843) William Thackeray described the workhouse as 'a large Gothic building'. In the same year a new courthouse was built to deal with the increase in crime as a direct result of increasing poverty. Few predicted that things would only get worse.

The Great Famine, caused by potato blight, began to take effect in 1845, but its long-term consequences were not immediately recognised. The Famine would affect every part of society, but most of all the small farmers and labourers, who depended on farming for survival. This was not a famine in the true sense, for there was plenty of food being produced in the country. However, the small tenant farmers and labourers were totally dependent on the potato for food, and once this crop failed they had no money to purchase other foods or to pay their rent. At the beginning of the Famine in 1845 and in 1846 many landlords reacted with compassion by reducing or deferring rent, and others provided funding to alleviate the starvation. George Browne, third marquess of Sligo, according to *The Telegraph* in 1846, had 'so humanely and so timely come to the aid of those who "to beg were ashamed, and to work were not able". Oh! if appeals to the charity of our contiguous landlords will be of no avail, let at least this powerful example be not lost upon them.'

In an effort to restrict the numbers seeking admission to the workhouses a scheme known as Outdoor Relief was introduced, which carried out public works such as building roads, bridges and drainage systems in return for food rations or wages. Charities were also organised, including the Westport Trade Industrial Society, which employed many throughout West Mayo. However, by 1847 there was no relief from famine, and the plight of the poorer farmers worsened. In that year the chaplain attached to the Westport workhouse consecrated an old quarry at the edge of the town as a mass grave for those who died of fever.

Asenath Nicholson's *Lights and shades of Ireland* records some of the most vivid descriptions of scenes and events in Ireland during the worst years of the Famine. In 1847 Nicholson wrote: 'I found here, at Newport, misery without a mask; the door and window of the kind Mrs. Arthur wore a spectacle of distress indescribable; naked, cold and dying, standing like petrified statues at the window, or imploring, for God's sake, a little food, till I almost wished that I might flee into the wilderness, far, far from the abode of any living creature'.

In February 1847, during the height of the Famine, George Lynch, secretary of the Kilgeever Parochial Relief Committee, set up in Louisburgh to help victims, claimed: 'While writing the Committee Rooms are surrounded by human beings crying out for relief—some to Heaven to release them from their sufferings—constant application for coffins. They are burying the dead this week without any, in order to apply the price to the purchase of food.' In June 1847 many of the starving attempted to escape the misery and boarded a ship called *The Argyle*, anchored at Inishgowla between Newport and Westport,

TRAGEDY FOSSILISED

In March 1847, the worst year of the Famine, Fr MacManus, George Lynch and George Hildebrand of the Kilgeever Parochial Relief Committee wrote: 'this remote desolate parish, lying between barren, inaccessible mountains and the wild neglected shores of the Atlantic; containing a population of 12,000 persons, all of the cottier class, hitherto solely depending on the potato for food. This large population is now without one ray of earthly hope...So frightfully and rapidly have famine, fever and dysentry prostrated a hardy and healthy peasantry, that the spectral survivors who venture abroad from their mountain homes are beyond recognition of their acquaintances, whilst many a hundred athletic young men are now lying under the green sod, along the Killery Bay.' Today grass grows on the ridges and furrows, called 'lazy-beds', on the hillsides where potatoes had been planted over 150 years ago, fossilising the hardship and tragedy of the Great Famine.

which sailed for Quebec in Canada.

Asenath Nicholson wrote about an incident near Westport in 1848: 'A cabin was seen closed one day a little out of the town, when a man had the curiosity to open it, and in a dark corner he found a family of the father, mother and two children, lying in close compact. The father was considerably decomposed; the mother, it appeared, had died last, and probably fastened the door, which was always the custom when all hope was extinguished, to get into the darkest

Pl. 86—Lazy-beds at Killary Harbour.

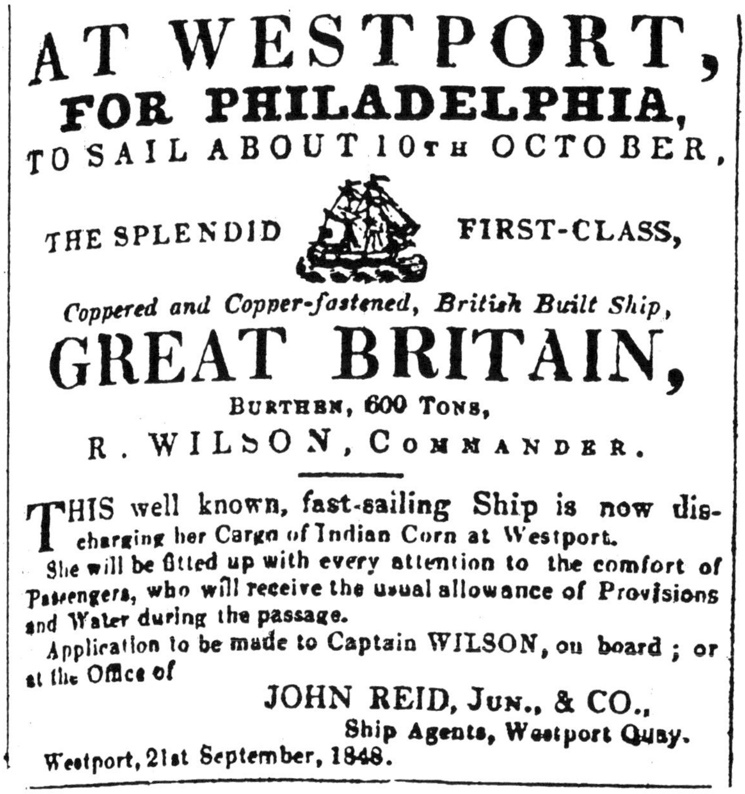

AT WESTPORT,
FOR PHILADELPHIA,
TO SAIL ABOUT 10TH OCTOBER,

THE SPLENDID   FIRST-CLASS,

Coppered and Copper-fastened, British Built Ship,

GREAT BRITAIN,
BURTHEN, 600 TONS,

R. WILSON, COMMANDER.

THIS well known, fast-sailing Ship is now dis-
charging her Cargo of Indian Corn at Westport.
She will be fitted up with every attention to the comfort of
Passengers, who will receive the usual allowance of Provisions
and Water during the passage.
Application to be made to Captain WILSON, on board ; or
at the Office of
JOHN REID, JUN., & CO.,
Ship Agents, Westport Quay.

Westport, 21st September, 1848.

EMIGRATION

On 27 September 1848 this advertisement appeared in *The Telegraph*. Typically merchants bringing food supplies to the ports of Ireland used their return sailings as an opportunity to fill their ships with passengers fleeing the famine in Ireland. These ships were rarely equipped to take passengers, with poor sanitation and overcrowding. Many died during the crossing, and the ships earned the nickname 'coffin ships'. They were generally the only affordable form of transport to Britain, Australia and the United States, where there was promise of economic salvation.

Fig. 22—
Advertisement in
The Telegraph, 27
September 1848.

corner and die, where passers-by could not see them. Such family scenes were quite common, and the cabin was pulled down upon them for a grave.'

Even during such human catastrophes there were those who saw capital gain. Some individuals working on behalf of the relief organisations were open to corruption. On 11 September 1848 John Carroll, who had been distributor of black bread to the destitute on behalf of the British Association, was tried at the Louisburgh petty sessions. *The Telegraph* reported that 'Carroll was fined in the highest penalty, or, in default of payment, to be imprisoned in Castlebar gaol, for having two pair of false scales, by which the paupers were deprived of a quarter of a pound'. Such cases appear to have been the exception rather than the rule; however, they do illustrate the fact that elements of Irish society other than the great landlords had little sympathy for the terrible suffering endured by their fellow Irish men and women.

SINCE THE FAMINE
Between 1841 and 1851 the population of Mayo fell by 29 per cent, one of the

TRAGEDY AT DELPHI

The picturesque Doo Lough Valley, then the fisheries of the marquess of Sligo, was the scene of a terrible tragedy that has come to symbolise for many the tragedy of the Famine itself. On 30 March 1849 Colonel Hogrove, guardian of Westport Union, and Captain Primrose, the Poor Law inspector, visited Louisburgh on a routine inspection of those claiming relief. They went on to Delphi Lodge in the heart of the remote Doo Lough Valley and requested that they be followed there by the poor, who would be inspected at eight o'clock the next morning. Those who were not at Delphi Lodge by 8.00a.m. would be struck off the list of those entitled to relief. The poor were so famished and exhausted that the sixteen-mile journey from Louisburgh during the cold night proved too much for many. According to an anonymous letter written to the *Mayo Constitution,* 'hundreds of these unfortunate living skeletons, men, women and children, might have been seen struggling through the mountain passes and roads for the appointed place...I have been told that nothing could equal the horrible appearance of those truly unfortunate creatures, some of them without a morsel to eat, and others exhausted from fatigue, having travelled upwards of 16 miles to attend this inspection'. At least five people died on the road, and it is believed that many more died shortly afterwards from the exertions of the journey.

largest reductions of any county. Many had died from starvation, many more had fled the country. The workhouse in Westport continued to house and feed the destitute for many years after the Famine, and in June 1850, even after the worst years, it had some 5000 inmates. The marquess of Sligo organised the

Pl. 87—Doo Lough Valley.

inmates into a workforce producing shoes and garments. There were 75 spinning-wheels in operation, producing the linen and flannel. The situation for many remained so bad that in July 1863 the entire small farming population of Kilgeever parish presented itself to the Westport workhouse and requested to be admitted, although only 95 out of the 600 could be facilitated. For nearly thirty years after the Famine the agents of landlords continued to evict many tenants in a concerted effort to clear the estates of unprofitable and undesirable small tenant farmers unable to pay their rents. In July 1848 *The Telegraph* reported the scene after several evictions near the half-way house in Islandeady:

> On Thursday we witnessed the wretched creatures endeavouring to root out the timber of the houses, with the intention of constructing some sort of sheds to screen their children from the heavy rain falling at the time. On Wednesday night there was a deluge of rain, the severity of which those poor creatures were exposed to in the open fields. Unfortunately for them, the pitiless pelting storm has continued ever since, and if they have survived its severity they must be more than human beings. Happy tenantry! Blessed with such kind hearted agents, whose desire manifestly is to give them as much fresh air as possible—and, to facilitate their procurement of food, send them forth to 'EAT GRASS'!

The long-term effect of famine and emigration was that the countryside changed dramatically: entire villages and communities disappeared and the agricultural economy continued to collapse. Emigration continued long after the Famine ended, and it has been estimated that in the parish of Kilgeever alone the population fell from 2200 families in 1846 to 600 families in 1900. Towards the end of the nineteenth century, land reform movements such as The Irish Land League, founded by Mayo-born Michael Davitt, successfully fought to secure fixed rents for tenants and to prevent landlords evicting people indiscriminately. Subsequently, the movements sought funding to allow tenants to purchase their farms. On 8 June 1879 Michael Davitt and Charles Stuart Parnell (the 'Uncrowned king of Ireland'), leader of the Home Rule party, spoke at a huge meeting at Westport in their quest for land reform.

As a youth, Major John MacBride attended this meeting. MacBride, born at Westport Quay, had moved to Dublin later in life, where he became an active member of the Irish Republican Brotherhood, a secret organisation that sought Irish independence. In 1899 MacBride, nicknamed 'Redhead', led an Irish brigade into battle against the British army in the Boer War in South Africa. Shortly afterwards MacBride went to Paris, where he was introduced to Maud Gonne, an avid Irish nationalist who had long rejected the obsessive advances of the great Irish poet William Butler Yeats. They later married at the Church of St Hoonoré d'Eylau in Paris but divorced in 1905. In 1916 MacBride became one of the leaders of the Easter Rising in Dublin, for which he was

DISTRESS IN THE WEST

This woodcut, 'A touch of nature: scene at an eviction on Clare Island', accompanied an article entitled 'The distress in the west of Ireland', published in *The Illustrated London News* on 10 April 1886. The woodcut is based on a sketch by Claude Byrne, who travelled with relief workers bringing 'seed potatoes, meal, and small gifts of money, to the famishing people'. The illustration shows a member of the Royal Irish Constabulary consoling the child of a family he had been ordered to evict.

A GHOSTLY TESTAMENT

Tumbled-down cottages are a ghostly testament to the extreme hardships of farming in the nineteenth and early twentieth centuries in West Mayo. In many places entire villages have vanished since the Great Famine. Emigration has gradually drained the life from this once-thriving and energetic rural landscape. Only in recent years have people and prosperity slowly begun to return to this part of the world.

Pl. 88— Abandoned farmhouse at Formoyle.

executed by the British army. He was buried with the other rebel leaders in a common grave at Arbor Hill in Dublin. This is a fitting point at which to conclude this chronicle of the history of West Mayo, for the 1916 Rising ushered in a new era, with dramatic changes for the entire island.

GUIDE TO THE MONUMENTS

Please remember that most archaeological sites are on private lands, and the landowners may wish to have that privacy respected. Always seek permission from the landowner before visiting a site.

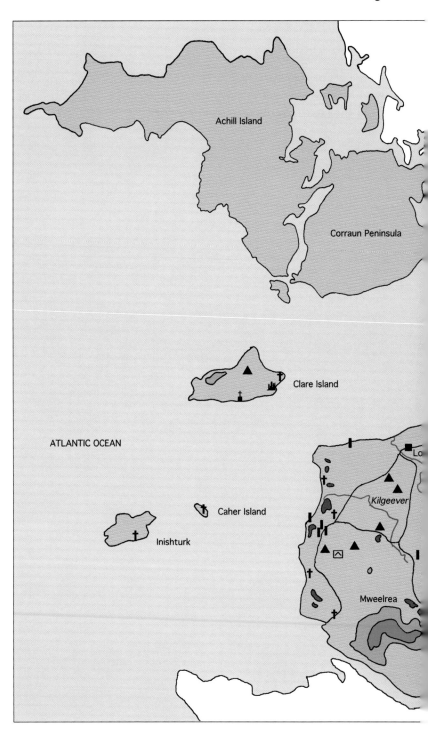

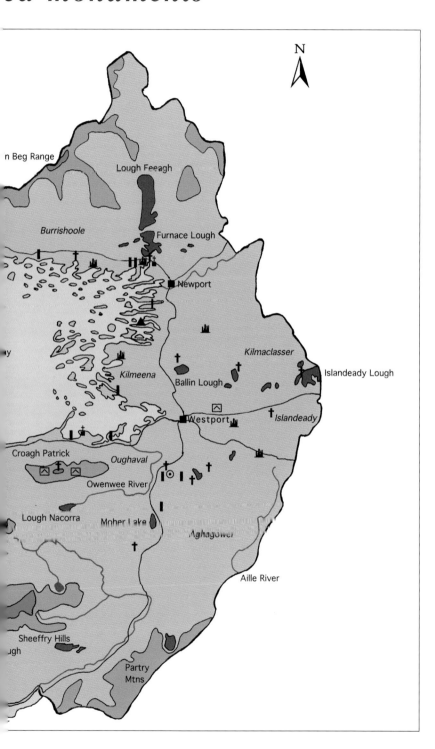

N

abbey
burial cairn
castle
church site
megalith
rock art
standing stone

Megalithic tombs

Aillemore

At Aillemore, on the eastern side of the Devlin hills, overlooking the valley of the Bunleemshough River is a fine court tomb known locally as *Leaba Dhiarmaid agus Gráinne*. The gallery is 4m long and is oriented east-south-east/west-north-west. At the east end is the entrance, which is an arrangement of stone sill and jambs. The gallery is divided into two chambers by another sill and jamb arrangement, and much of the corbelled roofing of high-pitched slabs is still in place. This roofing is partly retained by the surrounding oval cairn 16m long (east–west), 14m wide and 1.5m high. At the back (west) end of the cairn is a subsidiary chamber. The eastern half of the cairn has been refurbished, and there is no obvious evidence of a court. In 1871 the antiquarian George Kinahan was so impressed with the architecture of the tomb and its roofing that he thought he had discovered the rectangular version of the beehive hut, or clochaun.

Pl. 89—Devlin South wedge tomb.

Devlin South

On the bog-covered slopes of Devlin, overlooking the Atlantic coastline, are the

remains of a denuded wedge tomb, found as recently as 1994. The burial gallery of the tomb is *c.* 3m long, and the southern side is defined by a large slab 0.6m high and 1.7m long. Inside and parallel to this slab are three low stones, which may form an internal wall. A slab leaning inwards defines the northern side of the gallery. The entrance is at the west end, and there is a large slab that may have been a doorstone. There are traces of an irregular cairn 7.3m long (north–south) and 6.2m wide.

Feenune

At Feenune are the remains of a wedge tomb that has been partially dismantled. The tomb faces west, and at the east end the backstone is the only structural stone standing upright. The southern side stone leans inwards, and the northern stone slopes outwards. The roof appears to have been formed by two capstones, but these are displaced and have fallen to the north side and rear.

Formoyle

There are two court tombs in Formoyle. The tomb on the western slopes of Formoyle Hill is known locally as *Leaba Dhiarmaid agus Gráinne*. Unfortunately, it is poorly preserved and consists of a gallery 4.5m long (north-east/south-west)

Pl. 90—
Formoyle
court tomb.

represented by six stones. The southernmost stone was probably the backstone of the gallery. Only one stone, 0.45m high, defines the north-western side of the gallery. It is probable that there were originally two chambers within the gallery. The entrance to the gallery is defined by two jambs, each 1m high, set 0.5m apart. Adjoining the south-eastern jamb is a court stone 0.65m high. The tomb is surrounded by an oval mound 15m long (north-east/south-west) and 12m wide, surviving to an average height of 1.25m.

On the eastern slopes of Formoyle Hill is a large oval cairn of a court tomb 22.5m long (east-north-east/west-south-west), 18m wide and 0.7m high. The gallery has been dismantled, and only the entrance stones survive at the eastern end. Outside the entrance several small stones appear to form a horseshoe-shaped court 3m long (east–west) and 2.5m wide, open to the east, although given the small area enclosed and the small size of the stones it seems unlikely that they represent a court.

Pl. 91—
Lecarrow court
tomb, Clare
Island.

Lecarrow

Beside a pond on the slopes of Knockiveen Mountain on Clare Island are the remains of court tomb. The gallery of the tomb appears not to have been divided and is aligned east-north-east/west-south-west (5.6m long and 2m

wide). A number of the massive corbel slabs are still in evidence along the south-south-east. At the east end four stones survive of a court. The tomb is contained within an oval cairn 19m long and 12m wide.

Rosbeg

In Rosbeg are the remains of a court tomb known as 'Dermot and Grania's Bed', on a narrow promontory jutting into Clew Bay. The remains consist of a segmented gallery (5.3m long) oriented roughly east–west and surrounded by traces of a kerb. Tall jambs (that at the north is 2m high) and a septal stone divide the gallery into two chambers. There is no indication of the original extent or shape of the cairn. At the end of the nineteenth century an 'urn' was found in the east end of the monument. Also found, but now lost, were several flint objects, including a spearhead and three arrowheads. In the early 1930s the owner, Joe O'Malley Blackwell, and three local men excavated part of the site and found a polished stone axehead (now lost). However, when all of them were haunted by fearful dreams one night they ceased digging.

Srahwee

At Srahwee, near the shores of Lough Nahaltora, is one of the finest wedge tombs in Ireland. The gallery is 4.2m long, aligned roughly east-south-east/west-north-west, and is closed on the east end by a single backstone, while the entrance faces west-north-west. A septal stone 1.4m long x 1m high divides the main chamber, leaving a gap of 0.3m. The portico is currently defined by two stones on the south and one stone on the north and is open to the west-north-west. A second stone on the north has fallen into the portico. The flat roof stone was used as an altar during Penal times and has a primitive incised cross on the upper surface at the south-eastern end.

Tumuli and cairns

Carrowmacloughlin and Glencally

On the western shoulder of Croagh Patrick is a group of three cairns known as *Roilig Mhuire*, 'Mary's graveyard'. The cairns range from 6m to 12.5m across and from 1.7m to 1.9m high and form one of the stations of the medieval pilgrimage to Croagh Patrick; however, given the name 'graveyard' attached to the cairns, it seems probable that they are a cemetery of Early Bronze Age cairns.

Cashel

In Cashel is a grass-covered mound known as Turnincorragh, possibly deriving from the Irish *túirnín cuirreach*, 'the little hill of the marsh', or *túirnín corra*, 'the little hill of the serpent', from a lost folk tradition that it was inhabited by a terrible monster. The mound of earth and stone was originally *c.* 14m across and 1.8m high, but it was disturbed in 1954. For this reason it was partially investigated by Etienne Rynne in the same year. Near the centre of the mound a stone-lined cist had been exposed, which was excavated by Rynne. The cist measured 0.6m north-west/south-east x 0.3m and was *c.* 0.3m deep. It was divided into two compartments. The south-eastern compartment was empty, but the other contained some cremated bones and sherds of a vase-shaped food vessel pot. North-east of this cist, Rynne noted the outline of a second cist, also divided into two compartments, but this was not excavated. There was a tradition that at the beginning of the twentieth century a local clergyman excavated part of the site. Apparently a 'crock' was found, and reburied, and Rynne has suggested that the sherds of the food vessel may have been the same pot.

Derrygorman

At Derrygorman near Westport is a ring-barrow, consisting of a circular, flat-topped mound (4m in diameter, 0.15m high) enclosed by a shallow fosse (over 2m wide) and an outer earth and stone bank (*c.* 3m wide).

Devlin South

On the highest point of the Devlin hills above Killadoon, with dramatic 360° views, is a low cairn of stones *c.* 8m across. Some of the stones of the cairn were used by the Ordnance Survey in the nineteenth century to construct a pile of stones marking the highest point of the hill.

Letterkeen

At Letterkeen, excavations by Seán Ó Ríordáin and Máire MacDermott in 1950 revealed that in the early medieval period a ringfort had been built on top of an Early Bronze Age cemetery, which may have been covered originally by a mound or cairn. Five stone-lined graves were found containing the cremated human remains of about twelve individuals, representing adults and children. Cist 1 was a short rectangular cist containing the cremated remains of two adults and one child, accompanied by two vase-shaped food vessels. Cist 2 contained the cremated remains of two adults and an adolescent and was again accompanied by two vase-shaped food vessels. The two pots were placed inverted in the grave and covered small quantities of cremated bone. Cist 3 was divided into two compartments, one side containing the cremated remains of an adult and a child. A nearby pit contained the cremated remains of an adult accompanied by a pygmy cup. Nearby were several pits containing heavily burnt clay, charcoal and minute fragments of cremated bone, and these were interpreted as the remains of a crematorium.

Liscarney

Beside the tall standing stone at Liscarney is a small ring-barrow, consisting of a low mound enclosed by a ditch and outer bank, *c.* 17m across.

Murrisknabol

At Murrisknabol, near Murrisk, is a small mound (over 5m across) surrounded by sixteen kerb stones. Although this is probably not the mound in question, it is interesting that at the end of the seventh century Bishop Tírechán, in his Life of St Patrick, wrote that Patrick's charioteer, Totmael, died at Murrisk, on the plain between the sea and the mountain, where it is said that Patrick buried him and gathered stones together for his cairn.

Sheean

On the summit of Sheean Hill, overlooking Clew Bay and Croagh Patrick, is a large circular earth and stone mound (25m across, 2.7m high), known locally as *Siodhán an áil iarach* ('the fairy mound of the western cave'). This cave is probably a burial chamber within the mound. Directly north of the mound is an artificial pond (18m across) now choked up with tall grasses but once filled with water. It is possible that this is the remains of a ritual pond sometimes used in the Late Bronze Age for votive offerings.

Teevenacroaghy

On the eastern shoulder of Croagh Patrick, overlooking Lough Nacorra, is a cairn (7m across, 2.5m high). This may be the original cairn known as *Leacht Mionnáin* (possibly a corruption of Benain), and the name was later transferred to a new, almost insignificant cairn on the route now used by pilgrims ascending the Reek, the conical summit of the mountain.

Toberrooaun

In a hollow in a field at Toberrooaun is a small ring-barrow consisting of a domed circular mound over 13m across enclosed by a shallow ditch *c.* 1.5m across. There is no clear evidence of an outer bank.

*Pl. 92—Sheean
burial mound.*

Westport Demesne

Somewhere in Westport Demesne was a burial tomb of some kind that was excavated by Lord Altamont during the visit of Gabriel Beranger to the house in 1779. A plan of the monument survives, indicating that it was enclosed by a circle of around ten large stones, up to 1.8m high and 3.7m wide. At the centre several large stones supported a coffin-shaped roof stone, 2.1m long, 1m wide and 0.5m thick. Beranger gives an account of their endeavours:

> July 18th took a walk after dinner with my Lord to a large circle of stones, having a cromlegh in the centre, situated on his Lordship's ground on the sea-side; told him my notion, that they were burial places, and not temples, and proposed to get it opened, to which he consented, and fixed the next morning for that operation...After breakfast we set out with his Lordship and a large company of labourers, with all tools required to blast and remove large stones. The top stone of the cromlegh was broke, and also its pillars or supporters; but, as the work went on slowly, the men working unwillingly, murmuring, and saying it was a sin to disturb the dead, his lordship made them observe that the person buried there was not a

Christian, but a heathen, which, being dead, it was no sin to dig up his bones; to which they agreed, and fell to work with alacrity. At about four feet deep was found a kind of circle of paving stones, in the centre of which were bones which had been burned, some of them being sound in one end, but of a brown colour, and the other end like charcoal. The skull, though broke, was found, and, near it, a ball as round and of the size of a billiard ball, which, being washed and cleaned, appeared to us to be marble, which his Lordship kept. There were smaller bones found, and jaw bones of an animal with tusks, which we supposed was his favourite dog. The circle of stones which contained these bones was about two feet in diameter. Having thus assured ourselves that this monument was a mausoleum, and not a temple, we got the bones re-interred, and the grave covered, and one of the fragments of stone put over it.

Rock art

Boheh

A large outcrop of rock called St Patrick's Chair is almost totally covered in carvings, consisting primarily of cupmarks, many enclosed by one or more circles. There are also several unusual patterns known as keyhole motifs. From the stone there is a full view of Croagh Patrick, which led Gerry Bracken of Westport to examine whether there was a relationship between the rock art on the stone, the setting sun and Croagh Patrick. In 1987 he noted that from this site the sun can be seen to set on the summit of the Reek and, rather than disappear behind the mountain, roll down its shoulder as it sets on 18 April and 24 August. 24 August is St Bartholomew's Day, traditionally the first day of autumn and an important date for cereal producers. Perhaps 18 April was similarly important in prehistoric times. It has been suggested that the dates were used to celebrate the sowing and harvest seasons.

Standing stones

Askillaun

At Askillaun is a pair of parallel stone rows, 3m apart, known locally as *na clocha Fianna*, 'the stones of the Fianna'. This arrangement of two parallel rows is very unusual in Ireland. Both stone alignments are of granite boulders oriented north-north-east/south-south-west. The western alignment consists of three stones 1.22–1.8m high. The eastern alignment consists of five stones 0.95–1.15m high.

Boheh

Near the rock art on St Patrick's Chair in Boheh is a stone standing over 2m high known as the Long Stone. From this standing stone the rolling sun spectacle can also be seen, on 21 April and 21 August. Gerry Bracken and the late Patrick Wayman have pointed out that if 21 December is included these three dates divide a 366-day year into three equal parts of 122 days.

Cloonmonad

Currently situated at the centre of a traffic island in a housing estate in Westport is a tall standing stone, 1.8m high.

Cross

Beside the strand at Cross is an enormous standing stone, over 3m high, and a small companion stone just over 1m high, known as *An stoca mór agus an stoca beag*, meaning 'the big stone and the little stone'.

Derryheagh

On a knoll in the bog at Derryheagh, near the road from Louisburgh to Delphi, is a fine standing stone over 1.5m high. It has a curious feature in that surrounding its base is an arrangement of stones forming a small circle.

Devlin North

In Devlin, overlooking Inishturk and Caher Island, is a possible stone circle over 20m across. The circle is formed by upright stones, which are supported on the outside by an earth and stone bank. On the east side the enclosure was cut into the slope in order to support the largest upright stones of the circle, only one of which is now standing (over 1.7m high). The interior may originally have been hollowed to the bedrock, but it is currently filled with 0.05–0.2m of peaty soil. There is no evidence of an entrance, which may have been incorporated into the modern wall flanking the road that cuts the enclosure slightly at the west.

Formoyle

At Formoyle is a standing stone 1.2m high, with distant views of Doo Lough Valley to the south and Croagh Patrick to the east.

Killadangan

Beside the Westport–Louisburgh road, in a salt marsh, is a complex of standing stone monuments including a row of standing stones, a pair of standing stones, a stone circle and three individual standing stones. The stone row consists of four stones aligned north-north-east/south-south-west. The stones range from 0.45m to 1.2m high and increase in the height from north-north-east to south-south-west, rising in the direction of a niche, 2km directly south-south-west, in the eastern shoulder of Croagh Patrick. At 1.45p.m. on the winter solstice (21 December) the sun sets in this niche, directly in line with the stone row, and then disappears behind the shoulder of Croagh Patrick.

The stone circle, 75m south-west of the stone row, is a roughly circular arrangement of small stones enclosing an area 13m in diameter. This appears to be the remains of a well-defined stone circle marked on the 1837 OS six-inch map and probably consisted of orthostats or boulders. Today the site is much dismantled.

Killadoon

There are three standing stones in Killadoon. The largest and most impressive

*Pl. 93—Devlin
North stone circle.*

Pl. 94—
Killadoon
standing stone.

is near the site of the old schoolhouse, which has been demolished. It is over 2.7m high and 1.7m wide and is locally known as *An stoca mór,* 'the big stone'.

Knockalegan

The standing stones at Knockalegan have given their name to the townland: *Cnoc a liagain,* 'the hill of the pillar stones'. There are two stones that originally stood in a north-east/south-west line, but one has fallen. The south-western stone is 1.8m high and 1.1m wide (oriented north-north-east/south-south-west). The fallen stone (*c.* 2.1m long) lay *c.* 1.8m to the north-east of the other and may originally have stood to the same height. There is another standing stone in Knockalegan, on the shoreline overlooking a small inlet of Clew Bay.

Lanmore

There are two standing stones in Lanmore. The more impressive of these is St Patrick's Stone, which marks the route of *Tóchar Phádraig.* Today this pointed stone leans precariously to the north, but originally it would have stood to nearly 2.5m high.

Liscarney

A standing stone nearly 2m high and 1.8m wide (oriented north-east/south-west) is all that remains of a four-stone row. The landowner remembers that three further stones, about one-quarter of the size of the surviving stone, extended in a line directly north-east of the stone for a distance of *c.* 8m. These were cleared some years ago during land improvements.

Murrisk Demesne

At the foot of Croagh Patrick in Murrisk Demesne are three standing stones. Two of these stand close together in one field and are oriented on the summit of the Reek.

Rossgalliv

At Rossgalliv are two standing stones 1m apart, aligned north-east/south-west. The north-east stone is the larger, 1.5m high and 1.2m wide, and the other is 1.35m high and 0.9m wide. Both are 0.12m thick. There is a tradition that pins and rags were left at these stones, a custom normally reserved for seeking cures at holy wells.

Rusheen

At Rusheen near Carraholly, outside Westport, is a standing stone nearly 1.5m high, which, according to local tradition, was originally one of a pair.

Church sites

Aghadooey Glebe

In Aghadooey Glebe is a small graveyard known as Killeen, now enclosed within a square stone wall, that had been used as a potato garden. There are no longer any headstones, but there is a curious stone-built feature known as 'St Birroge's Bed', sometimes corrupted to 'St Barbara's Bed'. Incorporated into this feature is a slim stone incised with a cross. An area to the east of the square enclosure is known as the 'crush', probably a corruption of 'cross'. The OS six-inch map shows the line of two large outer enclosures around the site, of which there is no trace today.

To the south of the site is a holy well called Tobersool, from the Irish *tobar súl*, meaning the 'the well of the eyes', from the use of the water to cure eye ailments. The well is also sometimes called 'St Biorróg's Well'. According to one folk tradition, a British soldier fell in love with St Biorróg. When she asked him which part of her body he had fallen in love with, he replied her eyes, and she is said to have ripped them out and thrown them onto the ground, where the well then sprung up. According to custom, the stations at the well must be carried out before sunset on three days: Monday, Thursday and Monday, or Thursday, Monday and Thursday. Pilgrims stand at the foot of the well, facing west, and recite seven Our Fathers, seven Hail Marys and seven Glories; they then walk around the 'bed' seven times, reciting prayers of their own choice. The pilgrims then repeat all the prayers at the foot of the well.

These remains of an early church may be related to the name preserved in the neighbouring townland Kiltarnet, which derives from the Irish *Cill tSárnait*, 'the church of Sarnat [a female saint]'. There is a holy well in Kiltarnet dedicated to St Dominick and accredited with having a holy trout. The well is in fact a souterrain and it was probably originally within a ringfort, not a church site. It may have been attached to the Dominican friary at nearby Burrishoole, but the name 'Kiltarnet' appears to be older and may be related to the early remains associated with St Birroge.

Also in Aghadooey Glebe is a church known as Coollegrean church (the name derives from the Irish *cúl le gréin*, meaning 'back to the sun'). Local tradition holds that it was the site of a convent attached to the nearby abbey, but it seems more likely that it is the medieval parish church of Burrishoole. The building is long and narrow and required buttresses to support the west gable and the west end of the north wall. The west gable is covered in ivy but appears to have no features. Towards the west end of the south wall are a small slit window and a blocked-up doorway. It seems that this doorway was replaced by a door in the north wall, but this has since fallen and been replaced by a modern stile. At the east end the gable has fallen, and there is no trace of the east window. There is an aumbry in each of the north and south walls. A number of graves were found within the church. Unfortunately, there is no clear evidence of the date of construction of the church, especially given the lack of architectural pieces. However, the remains in the south wall of one side of a splay for a tall window, perhaps a lancet type, suggest a thirteenth-century date. Also, in the north wall are two putlog holes for holding timber scaffolding during construction, which are typical of late thirteenth- and early fourteenth-century buildings.

Aghagower

The church of Aghagower is mentioned as early as 700, when Bishop Tírechán, in his Life of St Patrick, claimed that it was founded by St Patrick for St Senach. Little is known about the church after this time, but it seems to have developed as the ecclesiastical centre of the kingdom of Umhall and to have received patronage from local rulers. In 1221 Diarmuid O Culechain died. He was a professor of history and writing and was honoured as a man who had more writings and knowledge than anyone that came in his own time. Listed among his writings are a Mass book that he wrote for his tutor, Diarmaid MacHerity, and his foster brother Gillapatrick, who were successive coarbs (church leaders) of Aghagower. O Culechain himself probably had connections with Aghagower and may even have received tutelage here. On 15 December 1231 Donn Cathaig, erenagh of Aghagower, died: he was described in the Annals of the Four Masters as 'settler of every dispute and covenant, a man of esteem and honour'. According to the Annals of Connaught, he died in 1233 and was 'a man reverenced by clergy and laity for his qualities of mind and body; the most generous bestower of cattle and food in his age; the protector of the wretched and the prosperous; an honour to his land and country; the reconciler of all disputes between his own household and the public in general'. This suggests that there may have been a dispute between the church and the local population during his term at Aghagower. In 1247 Benedictus Mag Oirechtaig (MacHerity), also erenagh of Aghagower, was treacherously slain at the festival of the Cross (3 May), by the son of Conor Rua O'Conor.

The church ruins are rectangular (17m east–west, 8m north–south) and late medieval in date. The western gable is no longer standing, but it is clear from the surviving foundations that there was once a west door. This door may be the only trace of an early church and was incorporated into a later building. Before this door was blocked up, Croagh Patrick would have been visible due west by anyone standing within the church. The eastern gable of the church is well preserved and has a fine Gothic window with a head carved at the base of one of the mullions. At the southern end of the eastern gable is a Gothic doorway that provides entry to a sacristy with three aumbries, the roof of which leaned against the outside of the eastern gable. At the northern end of the eastern gable is a vaulted chamber with access through a small entrance 1m above the floor level of the church: this may be a burial vault or may have been used to house a relic for pilgrims to see. The western gable is collapsed, and the original entrance is blocked up. There is a recessed round-headed doorway in the southern wall, dating to the late twelfth or early thirteenth century. There are also two ogee-headed windows in the south wall, one featuring a flat-hooded moulding with a carved human head.

West of the church are the remains of a round tower, probably dating to the late eleventh or early twelfth century. The external diameter of the tower is 5m, and today it stands almost 16m high. The original, round-headed door is at first-floor level and faces east, presumably in the direction of the original church. This door shows evidence of having been damaged by fire. There is a more recent entrance to the tower at ground level on the west side. Inside the tower are several rings of corbels, which would have supported the wooden floors. At the beginning of the nineteenth century, lightning destroyed the top of the tower, and the capstone is said to have landed half-a-mile to the south, on the hill of Tevenish. This capstone is now in the graveyard of the modern church and is one of only a small number of capstones from round towers surviving. The stone is conical (0.4m high) and has a small mortise hole at the top (0.05m deep), in which a small cross may have been inserted.

The Irish name of Aghagower is *Achaidh fobhair*, 'field of the spring'. Near the church are *Tober na nDeochaun* (recorded and translated by John O'Donovan as 'well of the deacons') and *Dabhach Patrick*, 'Patrick's Bath'. Built into the wall of *Dabhach Patrick* is a sheela-na-gig, which was probably moved here from the medieval church in the graveyard. Also near the church is *Leaba Phádraig*, 'Patrick's Bed'. Today this has been rebuilt, but for many years it consisted simply of a small rectangular area enclosed by a stone wall, and it was once an important place of prayer for pilgrims. Visiting the site in 1838, John O'Donovan wrote that he 'saw an old woman pray at this sacred spot, and I can never forget the enthusiastic glow of devotion to which her eyes gave expression, and I challenge all the philosophy of modern infidelity to produce an equal degree of religious consolation with that which she derived from prayers at this sacred shrine'.

In a field north-east of Aghagower are traces of a church known as *Teampull na bhFiacal* ('church of the tooth'), traditionally the site of a convent founded for Mathana by St Patrick. The pilgrim road from Ballintubber Abbey passed this church towards Aghagower. East of the church, on the approach to it along the pilgrim road, is a cairn known as *Leacht Tomaltaigh*. There is a tradition that a great man named Tomaltaigh came to Aghagower to laugh at the folly of the pilgrims, but God smote him for his infidelity and the cairn was raised as a monument of terror to infidels.

Boheh

In a grove of hazel trees near St Patrick's Chair is a small, unenclosed graveyard known as Killeen, with many low, uninscribed headstones. Within the graveyard is a small rectangular structure enclosed by a stone wall. On the inside of this wall are several upright slabs, including two cross-inscribed slabs. At the northern side is an entrance (0.48m wide) defined by two opposing upright cross-slabs separated by a low sill stone. The function of this feature is unclear, but it may have been built and used during the Penal period for services.

A short distance west of the graveyard is a holy well known as St Patrick's Well but currently dry. About 100m west of the graveyard is a small oblong cairn of stones known as the Priests' Grave, allegedly marking the grave of two priests, possibly killed during Penal times. At the north-western end of the cairn is a cross-inscribed slab.

Caher Island

Off the west coast, near Inishturk, is Caher Island, also known as *Oileán na Naomh*, 'the blessed island', and *Cathair Phádraig*, 'St Patrick's stone fort' (although sometimes the word *cathair* was used to describe a monastery). On the island are the ruins of a small fifteenth-century church with a tall slit window at the eastern end. Inside the church, below the window sill, is a low altar on which is an early medieval stone lamp and a large conglomerate stone known as *Leac na Naomh* that was formerly used as a cursing stone. The doorway at the west end of the church has a roughly pointed arch. The church appears to have been built using the stones of an earlier church. It stands within a small rectangular enclosure that may pre-date the present church.

Pilgrims made a *turas*, or round, of sixteen stations within and around the church. Many of the stations are marked by fine cross-slabs that may date to the seventh century. Among the stations is *Leaba Phádraig*, 'St Patrick's Bed', at the eastern end of the church. This consists of a cross-inscribed slab lying flat and a second slab, with a cross in false relief, standing upright at the west end. At the centre is a circular boss with a small incised cross-in-circle. These cross-slabs may mark the tomb of the founder of the church. Pilgrims would say a prayer here in Irish: 'My hard bed and pillow. Wretched for him, O Christ, who took possession of it!'.

Outside the eastern end of the church, near *Leaba Phádraig*, is a fine stone *leacht*, or altar, with a scatter of white quartz stones on top. There are three magnificent cross-slabs on top of the *leacht*. One features a Greek cross-in-circle and a pair of dolphins facing each other. It is believed that these remains belong to a hermitage site dating to the seventh century.

Capnagower

In Capnagower at the east end of Clare Island is a holy well known as *Tobar Féile Bríd*, 'the well of Brigid's Festival'. Stations were traditionally performed here

Pl. 95—Caher Island church.

Pl. 96—Caher Island cross-slab.

on 15 August rather than on St Brigid's Day, 1 February. According to Westropp, at the beginning of the twentieth century 'local tradition says that it harbours a holy fish, a mysterious trout, only to be seen by the most devout visitors'. South-west of the well is an irregular stone cashel 14.6m north–south and only 6.1m east–west at the north end. There is an entrance at the south. Much of the wall appears to have been rebuilt on older foundations. In the north-eastern corner is a small stone structure known as Labbabreed (deriving from the Irish *Leaba Brighdhe*, 'St Brigid's Bed'), perhaps the remains of a beehive-shaped hut. To the south of this is a pile of stones traditionally known as an altar, on which are a number of rounded beach stones. Westropp noted 'a couple of "anchor stones", large blocks, with a groove round them for a rope, doubtless votive from some fishing boat saved from destruction'. Westropp also recorded the traditional stations that were carried out here: 'the worshippers walking seven times sunward (i.e., with the right hand next the wall), round and just outside the cashel or enclosure. After this they go on their bare knees seven times round the labba and altar, inside it, emerging by a gap in the north wall, and finishing by prayers at the well.'

Carrowrevagh

At Carrowrevagh is a graveyard consisting of a roughly square artificial terrace (internal dimensions 21m east–west by 17m), built onto the hillside slope at the north and east. There are no obvious upstanding headstones, suggesting that

Pl. 98—
Carrowrevagh
cross-slab.

the site has not been used as a burial-ground for some time. In the south-west corner is a well-built drystone *leacht* of slabs with a rubble interior, roughly square in plan (2m east–west, 1.75m north–south and 0.85m high). On top of the *leacht* are a large quartz stone and eight rounded stones, including a spherical one (0.2m across). The south-eastern corner of the *leacht* is slightly collapsed, and a cross-slab has been dislodged. The slab (0.55m high) has a simple incised cross (0.25m high, 0.18m wide) with slightly bulbous terminals. The graveyard appears to be in the eastern quadrant of a large oval enclosure. Only part of this enclosure now survives along the south.

Cloonlaur

The graveyard in Cloonlaur townland south of Louisburgh is widely known as Killeen; however, the church may have given its original name to the neighbouring townland, Killadoon, *Cill an dúin*, 'church of the fort'. No trace of a church remains, but within the old graveyard is a circular raised platform that probably indicates an enclosure within which the church once stood. Among the many modern tombstones are several indications of the antiquity of the church. There is a large pagan standing stone (2.5m high), currently leaning precariously, which was Christianised sometime in the seventh century when a Maltese cross with a four-petalled marigold, enclosed by a double circle, was incised on it. This marigold forms an X, which may represent the first element of the chi-rho symbol. Also in the graveyard, now marking the grave of Revd David Lyons, is a cross-inscribed slab featuring a main cross at the centre surrounded by four smaller crosses. Designs on the lower part of the slab are currently obscured by a plaque in memory of Revd Lyons.

Croagh Patrick

The name Croagh Patrick was most commonly used in the late medieval period, although even as late as the twelfth century the mountain was frequently called *Crochán Aigli*. A poem in the Dindsenchas (Lore of Places) suggests that its earlier name was *Cruachán Garbois*. The meaning of these earlier names is not understood. In 1994 Gerry Walsh undertook an excavation that uncovered the remains of an early medieval building on the mountain summit. The building was rectangular (5.6m east–west x 3.5m north–south internally), with well-built drystone walls surviving to only 1m high. The south side was dug into bedrock, so that it appears to have been a partly sunken building. There was a doorway (0.68m wide) with a threshold flagstone at the eastern end of the building. Inside the entrance were two opposing post-holes that once supported an upright post on which to hang a door. The excavator suggested that the remains were of an early medieval stone church and argued that the untypical eastern doorway might be explained by the prevailing strong south-westerly winds on the mountain summit.

In 1838 John O'Donovan recorded another church on the summit, which he described as a 'little chapel called Tempull Patruig, which is sixteen feet long and eight broad at the east end, where the stone Altar is placed and only five at the entrance. Its east gable is eight and a half feet high, and many votive nails and rags are thrust in between the stones. By advice of my guide I left a rag of my own coat here, though God and Saint Patrick forgive me, I am but a weak

Pl. 99—
Church on
Croagh Patrick
during 1994
excavations
(courtesy of
Gerry Walsh ©).

believer.' This church cannot be found today and may have been situated where the modern church was built in 1905.

In 1838 Otway noted the presence of a stone wall enclosing the mountain summit. Today the wall is much collapsed and difficult to identify. However, excavations by Gerry Walsh in 1995 confirmed the presence of the wall. Finds consisted primarily of beads, including two of amber, one of yellow glass and four of blue glass. The function and date of the enclosure have not yet been confirmed.

O'Donovan gives the earliest description of stations performed by pilgrims on Croagh Patrick and records that the first station was a heap of stones known as *Leacht Mionnáin* or *Leacht Benain* (which he suggests refers to St Benigus) on the east side of the coned summit of the mountain. Pilgrims recited seven Our Fathers, seven Aves and one Creed while walking around the *leacht* seven times. They then climbed the cone of Croagh Patrick, the Reek, following the path named *Casan Phádraig*, 'Patrick's Way', and on reaching the summit recited seven Our Fathers, seven Aves and one Creed on their knees. The pilgims then entered *Teampull Phádraig*, kneeled before the altar and recited fifteen Our Fathers, fifteen Aves and one Creed. After this they walked barefoot around the summit fifteen times, then to the nearby *Leaba Phádraig* ('St Patrick's Bed') and finally to *Roilig Mhuire* on the western shoulder of Croagh Patrick, at the base of the cone of the mountain. Here the pilgrims walked around each of three cairns several times on their knees, reciting in each case seven Aves and one Creed.

The English travel writer William Thackeray, in his *Irish sketch-book* (1843), gives an interesting account of the climbing of the Reek on Garland Friday 1842. Thackeray's view of these Catholic Irish proceedings was generally not sympathetic, and his disapproving sarcasm is easily detected. It was general custom that after the climb the crowds of people assembled in festive mood at the base of the mountain. Thackeray found fifty tents in a field in the pouring rain and described the scene:

> Here was a great crowd of men and women, all ugly…Stalls were spread about, whereof the owners were shrieking out the praises of their wares— great, coarse, damp-looking bannocks of bread for the most part, or mayhap, a dirty collection of pigs' feet, and such refreshments. Several of the booths professed to belong to 'confectioners' from Westport or Castlebar, the confectionery consisting of huge biscuits and doubtful-looking ginger-beer— ginger-ale, or gingeretta, it is called in this country, by a fanciful people, who love the finest titles. Add to these, caldrons containing water for tay at the door of the booths, other pots full of masses of pale legs of mutton (the owner 'prodding' every now and then for a bit, and holding it up and asking the passenger to buy). In the booths, it was impossible to stand upright, or to see much, on account of smoke. Men and women were crowded in these rude tents, huddled together, and disappearing in the darkness. Owners came bustling out to replenish the emptied water-jugs, and land ladies stood outside in the rain calling strenuously upon all passersby to enter…Meanwhile, high up on the invisible mountain, the people were dragging their bleeding knees from altar to altar, flinging stones, and muttering some endless litanies, with the priests standing by.

Dadreen and Tallavbaun

Beside the road to Silver Strand, in the shadow of Mweelrea, is a tall stone pillar (1.88m high) with the outline of a Latin cross incised on the west face, which may date to the seventh century and probably marks the site of a lost church nearby. Nothing is known of the church, but there is an interesting tradition, recorded by James Berry, that there was once a little church in a gorge on the side of Mweelrea mountain:

> dating back to the earliest Christian times. This little church was roofed with stone on the principal of the arch, like St Dara's church off Carna, or that

of Ardfert in Kerry. Some distance from the little church there stood four rude stone crosses facing the four cardinal points, in consequence of which the gorge where the little church stood was called by the peasantry 'Maum na gress' or 'cress', the gorge of the crosses. There it stood, far removed from any habitation, some fifteen hundred feet above the vast plain: there it has stood since the sixth century, but tradition had forgotten the name of its saintly founder.

On a certain fine evening in summer time when the peasant girls from the numerous villages which lay at the foot of the great hill climbed towards the gorge in order to milk their cows which congregated there every evening, the little church stood there in solitary grandeur, but when the peasantry arose the next morning, the little church was standing on the green plain at the foot of the hill. There it stands like the House of Loretto, the wonder, the admiration and the pride of the natives who came in haste and amazement to gaze at the phenomenon, or miracle, rather, and the peasantry called the plain around the little church 'Dooya an thompal', or the sandy beach of the church.

It is uncertain whether the church originally on the side of Mweelrea in the story is that marked by the cross pillar at Dadreen. However, the reincarnated church 'Dooya an thompal' is almost certainly the remains of a church and graveyard still known as Templedoomore on the sands of Tallavbaun. In around 1950 the remains of a church could still be seen, but today the site has all but disappeared, destroyed by the ravages of the Atlantic Ocean. A gaming-piece and a spindle whorl were found here in the 1930s.

Doughmakeon

In the sand dunes of Doughmakeon on the Atlantic coast is a stone pillar with an incised Maltese cross. Some ogham markings were noted by Principal Rhys in 1898, although no trace of such markings remains today. It was recorded in the Ordnance Survey Name Books in 1838 that the nearby Lough Cahasy was 'called after a St Cathasach' and that a 'saint is said to have resided here, and stations are performed'. At this time John O'Donovan also recorded that there was a stone here called *Claidhimhín Chathasaigh*, 'Cathansach's little sword', that was used as a cursing stone. In the same year, Caesar Otway learned of this cursing stone and recorded that it was also called 'the stone of Duac McShaun', suggesting that it was situated in the townland of Doughmakeon on the north side of Lough Cahasy. This cursing stone may be the cross-inscribed pillar in the sand dunes here or a different stone nearby and now lost. All the evidence points to the probability that there was an early medieval church site in the sand dunes here that became inundated by the sands after it was abandoned.

James Berry recalled a rather fanciful story that there were 'three tall lintels or flags about five feet high', called the Swords of Casey, which 'since the days of the pagan ancestors slew some thousands of people'. In 1800 the archbishop of Tuam had them dug up and cast them into the middle of the lake, only to awake the next morning to hear that they were back in their original position on the shore of the lake. 'The Archbishop put on his full pontificals, took his crozier in his hand and marched down once more to Lough Casey. When he beheld the terrible pillar stones standing in the same spot he became enraged and ran towards them, smiting them with his Crozier until they fell. Then he took a sledge and smashed them into fragments, and taking the fragments into a boat, he rowed out to sea and cast them into the ocean where they sank beneath the dark waves and were never again seen on the shores of Lough Casey.'

Fahburren

The graveyard in Fahburren overlooking Clew Bay is called Killmacute or Killmacuffe in the *Book of survey and distribution* of 1641–1703. The name Killmacuffe may be related to the name of the neighbouring townland Killeencoffey. The graveyard is enclosed by a modern rectangular stone wall, in which may be the foundations of the church. There are many headstones but no obvious trace of any cross-slabs; however, there is a bullaun stone. To the west of the modern graveyard are the remains of a small circular enclosure 21m across, defined by a collapsed stone wall. Both this enclosure and the graveyard are surrounded by a much larger enclosure, best preserved along the north, where it consists of two closely set, stone-faced terraces. Very little is known of the history of this site, but its large size suggests that this was once an important church, perhaps linked with the pilgrimage to Croagh Patrick.

Feenune

In Feenune are the remains of a small graveyard known locally as Killeen Beg, which was used in modern times as a children's burial-ground. The graveyard is a raised rectangular enclosure 15m north–south x 11.5m east–west. There is a stone pillar (1.15m high) with traces of an incised double circle, which may originally have had an incised cross that has since been weathered away. Recently found at the site by this writer was a small slab (0.7m long) with a small incised cross-in-circle.

Furgill

The site at Furgill is marked variously on the OS six-inch map as 'Gloonpatrick' and 'Milla Burial Ground'. At the higher, southern end of a large oblong enclosure are two irregular terraces cut into the slope. The terrace at the southern end is the larger, and there are many low, uninscribed headstones scattered about. Immediately below this is a second terrace, at the east end of which is a small cairn marked on the OS six-inch map as an 'Altar'.

On the western side of the enclosure, perhaps on an approach up to the large terrace at the southern end, is an earthfast boulder with a slightly oval bullaun. The bullaun lies in the graveyard where 'St. Patrick's Well' is marked on the OS six-inch map. However, this may misname the dried-up well at the bottom of the slope. The well consists of hollow area enclosed by a crude drystone wall. The bullaun may explain the name 'Gloonpatrick', *glúin Phádraig*, meaning 'Patrick's knee', presumably from a legend explaining that the hollow was made by St Patrick's knee.

Glaspatrick

On the foothills of Croagh Patrick, beside the stream Glas Patrick (*glaise Phádraig*, 'Patrick's Stream'), are a church and graveyard that take their name from the stream. The small graveyard is largely overgrown with briars that engulf the remains of a small church. The west gable of the church is gone, and the east gable has been reduced to the foundations. The north and south walls are the best preserved and stand between 1.7m and 2m high. Unfortunately, there are no surviving architectural pieces such as fragments of windows to indicate a date for the construction of this church. However, its small size and the large stones used in its construction suggest that it belongs to the early medieval period, perhaps the twelfth century.

Islandeady

On the side of a hill projecting into Islandeady Lough are the church and graveyard of Islandeady, which gave the parish its name. As the name suggests, the hill was probably originally an island in the lake. Today the site is joined to the mainland by a modern road, probably on the site of an earlier causeway. In 1838 Thomas O'Conor of the Ordnance Survey recorded a local tradition that the church takes its name from its founder Eidin, whose grave was then shown on the north side of the east gable of the church. More recently it has been suggested that 'eady' might be a corruption of the Saxon name Edgar. However, there is no firm archaeological evidence that this was an early

foundation. The church is a late medieval building (17m east–west x 7m north–south). Towards the west end of the south wall is a fine Gothic doorway, decorated externally with a rosette and a human head on either side of the hood. Inside the door is a holy water stoup. The west gable has a plain but attractive ogee-headed window. The east window is a tall, two-light ogee-headed window, decorated with spandrels externally. The base of the mullion is decorated on either side with beautiful crosses and unique carved images of a switch-line tracery window and a trefoil-headed window.

Pl. 100—Islandeady church.

Kilbree Upper

The graveyard at Kilbree Upper takes its name from St Brigid. Throughout the graveyard are many low headstones, and the site was used as a children's burial-ground until 1929. Towards the east end is a square altar, 1.8m across and 0.45m high. West of this are the ruins of a small church, probably an oratory built in the twelfth century. The church measures only 5.1m east–west and 3.4m north–south, and the walls have largely collapsed, surviving to only 1m high, except the north-western angle, which is 1.8m high. At the west end of the church are the lower levels of a door, 0.8m wide. The windows have collapsed, but among the rubble are two round-headed lintels of windows. These typically date to the twelfth century, and the large stones used in the construction of the church also suggest an early date. In a field south of the graveyard was a holy well dedicated to St Brigid that was filled in sometime in the nineteenth century. The water of the well was attributed with the power to cure sores and warts.

Kilbride

Today there are no traces of the early church foundation in the graveyard at Kilbride, except for a bullaun stone. However, the name associates the site with St Brigid and suggests that there had been a church here since the early medieval period. According to John O'Donovan, in 1838 pilgrims to St Marcan's church at Rosclave did not go past the church at Kilbride or 'touch any places sacred to St. Brigid, lest the efficacy of their turas should be rendered null and void', because of a legendary argument between the two saints.

Kilgeever

Situated on the south-western slopes of Kinknock, this church was traditionally where pilgrims stopped to perform stations on the *turas* from Croagh Patrick to Caher Island. The name Kilgeever is not readily explained, but it has been suggested that 'geever' represents a personal name. Kilgeever could also derive from the Irish *Cill gaobhar*, meaning 'the near church'. Nothing is known of the history of this site, even though it appears to have been the parish church throughout the late medieval period.

The church is rectangular (16.6m east–west, 5.1m north–south) with a twelfth-century round-headed window in the eastern gable. Towards the eastern end of the church are two aumbries in the walls. Towards the western end of the south wall is a fifteenth-century door with a pock-dressed arch and a draw-bar hole to secure a beam that locked the door. In the soffit of the door is the impression of the wicker frame used to support the arch during its construction. The west gable is reduced to grass-covered foundations; however, when O'Donovan visited the site in 1838 it was still standing and he described and sketched a blocked-up flat-lintelled doorway: 'It is now 5 feet 4 inches high and 2 feet 4 inches broad, and built of rude slatey flags'.

Also in the graveyard are two cross-slabs. One is a small pillar stone standing east-south-east of the church, featuring a cross with dovetail terminals, formed by a deep, V-sectioned groove. A second slab has a similar cross incised on it.

Originally from this site (now in private possession) is a miniature cross-shaped stone, featuring an incised Latin cross. At the intersection of the arms is a cupmark enclosed by an incised circle. The cross has trumpet-shaped terminals.

In the north-west angle of the present graveyard enclosure is a spring well, above which is a modern stone monument. The well is marked on the OS six-inch map as 'ToberRiganDomnaig', meaning 'Our Lord's well of the Sabbath'. O'Donovan recorded that pilgrims came to the well on 15 July, the Festival of the Twelve Apostles.

Pl. 101—Kilgeever holy well c. 1890 (Wynne collection, courtesy of Gary Wynne ©).

Kilmeena

Little is known about the church at Kilmeena, although it gives its name to the parish and probably served as a parish church in the late medieval period. In 1838 John O'Donovan of the Ordnance Survey recorded the tradition that the church takes its name from St Meena, although there is no record of such a saint or ecclesiastic. Seventeenth-century forms of the name are Killemyna and Killminc. O'Donovan recorded a local tradition of how the parishes of Kilmeena and neighbouring Kilmaclasser were divided. The two saints Meena and MacGlaise moved 'in a straight line towards each other on their knees and wherever they met was to be a point of separation. Saint Meena, however, who had all the roguery of a primitive and modern saint got up on his feet and took to racing, which when Saint Mac Glaise perceived he became so wroth that he stooped down to take up a stone to hit the other with it, on the head. But his hand was stuck to the stone! Recognising that this was the intention of Providence he agreed that Saint Meena was right in playing this piece of roguery upon him, and consented to fix the boundary between the parishes there.'

All that survives of Kilmeena church is the steeply pitched west gable, standing over 5m high. In the gable is a round-arched door (2m high), with impressions in the mortar of plank-centring used in its construction, typical of the thirteenth century. There is a draw-bar hole within the wall. No features of an earlier date survive at the site.

Knappaghmanagh

At Knappaghmanagh are the interesting remains of an early church site with fine views of Croagh Patrick. The remains of a large oval enclosure (72m north–south, 56m east–west) define the sacred ground of the church. In the southern quadrant is a raised area (16m across) marked as a 'Children's Burial Ground' on the OS six-inch map. There are several low, uninscribed headstones scattered around. However, on one triangular slab is an equal-armed cross enclosed by a double circle. In each quadrant is a small cupmark. From the base of the outer circle three incised lines emanate, forming the legs of a human figure. Directly above the outer circle enclosing the cross is an incised circle, enclosing incised eyes, nose and mouth, forming the face of a human figure, above which is an incised design representing hair. On either side of the head of this figure is a cupmark. On the bottom left side of the slab is an incised Greek cross enclosed by a diamond. The early maps mark the site of an altar at the south end of the enclosure, but this has since been removed. Apparently the altar was then built up against the inside of the enclosure wall and was said to have been used as a Penal altar. On a low, tree-covered knoll to the south of the enclosure is an earthwork previously known as 'Fert', but its significance is not understood.

Lankill

Lankill takes its name from the Irish *Lann Cille*, 'enclosure of the church', of which there are traces, including the remains of a stone-built entrance that has been mistaken by some for a megalithic tomb. The field is known as *Gort na Manach*, 'the field of the monks'. The graveyard is within a grove of hawthorns and is one of the most striking in the country, with dozens of low, uninscribed headstones, a haunting reminder of days gone by. This was used from Penal times until the middle of the twentieth century as a children's burial-ground, but the graveyard may also have been used for adults throughout the Penal period. Within the graveyard is a drystone altar, probably used during the Penal period, which may be built on an earlier altar. On top of the altar is a stone with a simple cross carved on either side. On the east side of the graveyard is 'St Brendan's Well'—a bullaun stone—the waters of which were used for curing falling sickness. To the north of the graveyard is a tall stone pillar (2.6m high), perhaps a prehistoric standing stone, with an elaborate cross carved on either side. The cross features concentric circles that were previously believed to be of pagan origin; however, this type of decorative motif is known elsewhere in a Christian context. To the east of this stone are the grass-covered foundations of a small building, probably an early church.

Moyna

There is no evidence of a church site at Moyna, but there is a holy well traditionally associated with St Brendan. Richard Pococke, in his tour of 1752, wrote that the well was also called O'Malley's Well, 'concerning which there is a tradition in the Country, that a female child of this family, being dipt in it became a Male, which was probably some trick in order to secure the estate of the family in that Child'.

Local folklore still tells that the wife of an O'Malley chieftain escaped a slaughter on Clare Island and landed in Kilmeena, where she gave birth to a female child. Bearing the child in her arms, she met St Brendan and asked him to baptise her child. Her husband and other male members of the family had been killed, and she mourned that she had not given birth to a son. Brendan took pity on her and pulled up a flagstone, whereupon the well formed and he dipped the child into the water. On this, the sex of the baby was changed. This ensured the continuation of the O'Malley tribe, and from that baby boy all the O'Malleys claimed descent.

Oughaval

The church at Oughaval appears to take its name from the Irish *Nua Congbáil*, meaning the 'new foundation'. The church ruins are of late medieval date, and it may have been refurbished in the late seventeenth or early eighteenth century. A stone with the inscription 'Pray for the soul of Peter Browne who caused me to be made 1723' can be found in a nearby ringfort at Carrownalurgan. This probably came from an altar commissioned by Browne, who was the last Catholic in the family. It is possible that the altar stone originally came from the church at Oughaval, which may have fallen into disuse after Peter Browne's death in 1724. His son John Denis Browne was converted to Protestantism and built a Protestant church in the grounds of Westport House. The west end of the church at Oughaval is an annex reserved for the burial of wealthy families, and the entrance to this annex is an early twelfth-century flat-lintelled doorway with traces of roll-moulding. The door, over 2m high, appears to have been reused and reconstructed in its present position and must have belonged to an earlier church at the site.

The church has strong associations with St Colum Cille, and it is recorded that a member of the O'Malley family was slain in the church by the son of Donnell O'Dowda in 1131. O'Dowda was killed three months later by his own spear 'through the miracle of Columcille'. In 1838 John O'Donovan of the Ordnance Survey met an elderly man here who told him of a stone called *Leac Cholumb Cille* that the people used to wish each other bad luck, but the stone had been broken by order of the local priest.

Outside the graveyard is a dried-up holy well that has long been accredited with harbouring sacred trout with curative powers. William Thackeray in 1842 was told 'In the holy well lives a sacred trout, whom sick people come to consult, and who operates great cures in the neighbourhood. If the Patient sees the trout floating on his back, he dies; if on his belly, he lives; or *vice versa.*'

In the same year Mr and Mrs Samuel Carter Hall on their tour of Ireland were told the story of how these trout were marked when they had been interfered with: 'an heretical soldier once took home the trout looked upon as sacred, and placed it on a gridiron to cook from hence it escaped, and was found next day in the waters of the well, with the mark of the hot bars on its side. The fish (there are always two), which are very small and dark, hide beneath the stone wall…and they are lured out by a few worms thrown into the water, which they dart forward to catch, and as rapidly retire.'

The well has strong associations with St Colum Cille, but a different story explaining its origin was told to the Halls: 'St. Patrick being very tired, after mounting the hill [Croagh Patrick], to bless Connemara and the Joyce's County, and very thirsty, wished for a drink—instantly, out sprang the water from the holy well. When the saint was satisfied, however, it retired into its rocky recess; and many centuries afterwards, a good priest, poking about the neighbourhood, took notice of a small stone with a cross upon it; this stone he raised, when out gushed the clear stream.'

North of the road is a small modern graveyard, which appears to have a more modern association with St Patrick. The French tourist de Latocnaye, who travelled around Ireland from 1796 to 1797, wrote 'There has been specially pointed out to me a large stone on which there are two fairly deep holes, and the inhabitants venerate it as having been used by St Patrick, the holes having been worn by his knees while he prayed. Catholics and Protestants here made use of the same building for services while their churches were being built.' This graveyard north of the road is known as Gloonpatrick, *glúin Phádraig*, 'Patrick's knee'. In this part of the graveyard is a stone with two large but shallow hollows, presumably the stone mentioned by de Latocnaye, but the hollows may be natural.

Rosclave

At Rosclave are the remains of an early church site on a peninsula called 'The Green' projecting into a little bay known as St Marcan's Lough. Folklore has it that St Brigid cursed St Marcan after an argument and prayed that the sea would inundate his house. Nearby was a church called *Teampall Marcain*, which was demolished some years ago. The adjoining ground was called *Garrdha Teampaill*. There were also a stone *leacht* and a burial-ground on the grassy peninsula, but now nothing can be seen. On the nearby foreshore, exposed only at low tide, is a small, seaweed-covered cairn of stones (3.1m east–west, 2.3m north–south, 0.35m high), which is said to be a station and has the 'cure for man or beast'. A holy well known as Tobermarcan is situated nearby, and traditionally stations were performed here on Sundays. In 1838 O'Donovan reported that pilgrims still came here on 1 August, bringing their cattle to the well to be cured of various diseases. Other traditions claim that it was usual to swim sick cattle and horses across the bay. Stations were also performed at the well and altar on 8 June, the Fair Day of Newport, to pray for a successful livestock market.

The traditional stations involved going barefoot to the *leacht* in the low tide area, kneeling facing east and saying seven Paters, seven Aves and seven Glorias. Next, the pilgrims walked sunwise around the cairn seven times, each time repeating a Pater, an Ave and a Gloria. Then the pilgrims returned to the starting point and, kneeling, offered seven more Paters, Aves and Glorias, finishing with the Apostles' Creed. This pattern of prayer was carried out again at both the altar and the well.

Roskeen

Beside the seashore at Roskeen is a graveyard on a raised mound, and near the shore are an altar and holy well. There are no traces of a church in the graveyard, and no other objects of interest, but this is probably the site of an early church foundation. The well is sometimes called *Tobar a Chillín* and is dedicated to St Brendan. Pilgrims carried out stations here on the saint's day, 16 May, which involved walking around the altar and well seven times while repeating seven Our Fathers and seven Hail Marys. The water from the well is salty, and it was usually taken away in bottles for cures. According to one tradition, the well used to be in the graveyard, but something wrong was done at it and it went out to sea. St Brendan prayed and brought it back, but he could not bring it further than the edge of the sea. Another tradition tells that when a plague threatened to devastate the region the local people gathered at the church here and prayed *Bléanainn míor-úilteach idir sinn agus phláigh* ('Brendan of the miracles between us and the plague'). St Brendan heard their prayers and in turn prayed for the safety of his people. God granted his request and the plague did not enter the region.

Rushbrook

In the townland of Rushbrook, near the shores of Clogher Lake, are a church and graveyard called Kilmaclasser, which derives from the Irish *Cill Mhic Laisre*, meaning the 'church of MacLasser'. This was a common personal name in the early medieval period and literally means 'son of flame'. The ivy-covered church ruins are of a long rectangular building (19m east–west x 4.1m north–south). The door has fallen but appears to have been midway along the southern wall, and no windows survive. Indeed, there are no architectural clues to the date of this building, but given its unusual length it probably had more than one phase of construction, possibly dating to the late medieval period, when it was used as a parish church. There is no trace of an enclosure immediately around the church, but a stone wall forming an outer circle *c.* 85m across encloses the whole graveyard. (See Kilmeena for a legend on how that parish became divided from Kilmaclasser.)

Abbeys

Burrishoole

On the shores of Clew Bay near Newport are the ruins of Burrishoole Abbey, a Dominican friary dedicated to St Mary and founded by Richard de Burgo (Burke) in 1470. Richard entered the order himself and lived there until his death in 1473. Permission from the Pope was not sought for the foundation of the abbey, an oversight for which the community faced the threat of excommunication, but in 1486 the Pope instructed the archbishop of Tuam to

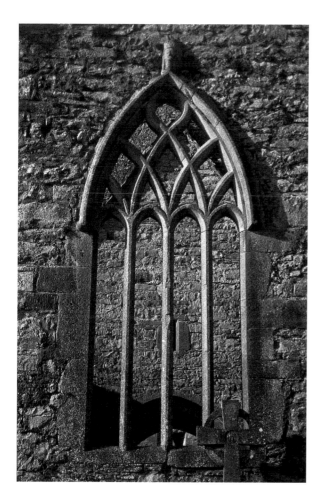

*Pl. 102—Burrishoole
Abbey, tracery window.*

grant the friars absolution. Long after the Dissolution of the Monasteries by Henry VIII a small community of monks continued to occupy the site. However, in 1580 the abbey was fortified and garrisoned by Sir Nicholas Malby, the English governor of Connacht. Malby described it as 'an abbey standing very pleasant by a river side, within three miles from the sea, where a ship of 500 tons may lie at anchor in low water. It hath a goodly and large lough on the upper part of the river, full of great timber, grey marble, and many other commodities, and not without great store of good land, both arable and pasture. Specially it hath a very plentiful iron mine, and an abundance of wood every way. Towards the sea coast there lieth many fair islands, rich and plentiful of all commodities. There cometh hither every year likely about fifty English ships for fishing. They have been before this time compelled to pay a great tribute to the O'Malleys.' In 1612 there was a ward at Burrishoole with a constable and ten warders. In 1653 the abbey was occupied by Cromwellian troops.

According to the will of Peregrine O'Clery (one of the scribes of the Annals of the Four Masters), he wished to be buried at Burrishoole upon his death (in 1664). The friars appear to have abandoned the site by 1779, when Gabriel Beranger and Angelo Maria Bigari visited and painted the ruins. According to Edward Ledwich in Grose's *Antiquities of Ireland* (1796) a great festival was held here on 4 August (St Dominick's Day). Mr and Mrs Samuel Carter Hall in their 1842 tour recorded that:

> Here, tradition states, the skull of Grace O'Malley was formerly preserved, and valued as a precious relic. One night, however—so the legend goes— the bones of the famous sea-queen were stolen from their resting-place, and conveyed, with those of thousands of her descendants, into Scotland, to be ground into manure. The theft was of course perpetrated in secret and in the night-time; if the crew had been seized by the peasantry with their singular cargo, not a man of them would have lived to tell the tale; for the Irish regard with peculiar horror any desecration of the grave-yard. It is said, however, and believed by many, that, by some miraculous interposition the skull of the brave lady was conveyed back to its nook in the Abbey-wall. The honour of having contained it is claimed also by Clare Island...In neither place is any such relic to be now met with.

The ruins consist of a church with a south transept and the remains of a cloister. At the west end of the church is the doorway, inside of which is a fine free-standing font. The church is divided into a nave and a chancel. At this division is a fine tower, in the vault of which can be seen two holes for the ropes of the bells. Access to the tower is gained by a winding stone staircase. On the east side of the tower the pitch of the roofline over the chancel is clearly marked. Underneath the tower on the north side are the remains of stone seating, lit by a two-light ogee-headed window. At the east end of the chancel is a fine switch-line tracery window, below which is the altar. At the apex of the window on the outside is the carved head of an abbot. In the nave, in the shadow of the tower, is the grave of Father Manus Sweeney, who was hanged for his part in the 1798 Rebellion. Extending to the south is a transept lit by a fine tracery window at the south end. Beneath this window is a piscina niche, with a Gothic arch and a bowl with a drainhole for washing the communion vessels, beside which is an aumbry for their storage. In the east wall of the transept is the altar tomb marking the grave of David Kelly junior, who died in 1623, and his wife Annabel Barrett.

In the north wall of the chancel a small Gothic doorway gave access to the

cloister, dormitories and other domestic buildings that originally stood to the north of the church. These buildings have largely disappeared, although the outer wall of the cloister survives along the north and west and has several gun-loops, probably inserted by the garrisons here at the end of the sixteenth century. The buildings attached to the cloister have almost disappeared, except along the east, where the chapter room and refectory were probably situated. Above these was the dormitory. In 1916 a fifteenth-century bronze seal was found embedded in one of the dormitory windows.

Pl. 103—Clare Island Abbey c. 1976 (courtesy of Dúchas The Heritage Service ©).

Clare Island

On Clare Island are the remains of an abbey that was attached to the Cistercian foundation of Abbeyknockmoy, Co. Galway, but little else is known about the history of this site. The building consists simply of a nave and chancel divided by an arch. The chancel is spanned by a fine barrel vault, and a staircase in the south wall leads to the domestic chamber above the vault. There is an annex to the north wall of the chancel, which at ground floor served as a sacristy, and at the first floor is another domestic chamber furnished with a garderobe. The chancel is lit by only two slender ogee-headed windows and must always have been dark. This may be one reason why the paintings that decorate the walls and ceiling of the vault are so well preserved. Recently these paintings, which rarely survive at Irish monasteries or churches, were painstakingly conserved. Two phases of painting were identified when the plaster fell away and exposed an earlier layer of plaster that was also decorated with paintings. Scenes include a cattle raid; a knight dressed in chain mail on horseback; wolves attacking stags; musicians; dragons; and griffins. The vault was painted with false ribs, which divided the surface into sixteen triangular areas. In the north wall of the chancel is a beautiful canopy tomb, in which are faint traces of a representation of the Crucifixion painted on the back wall. The canopy tomb is traditionally the burial place of Grace O'Malley, although it is probably fifteenth-century in date. The tracery of the tomb was painted in shades of black and red. A curious feature is that on the wall between this tomb and the east end wall of the chancel are faint traces of a replica of the canopy tomb, also painted in red and black directly onto the wall. Attached to the north wall is a plaque with the O'Malley coat of arms, probably dating to the seventeenth century.

North of the abbey is Tobarfelamurry, *Tobar Féile Muire*, 'Well of Mary's Festival'. This dedication probably derives from the fact that the abbey was attached to and served by Cistercian monks from Abbeyknockmoy, whose patron was Mary. The only evidence that this is the site of an early medieval foundation is a tall stone pillar (2.6m high) standing in the graveyard, which has a plain incised cross on its eastern face.

Caesar Otway visited the island and this church in 1838. He wrote that his guide took a skull from the eastern window of the church 'in the sides of which where the ears once were, holes had been made, and therein were inserted a pair of plain gold earrings—and this I was told was the skull of Grana Uaile'. He also wrote that after his visit the skulls and many other human remains in the graveyard had been stolen and brought to Scotland, where they were ground down and used as fertiliser. This is very similar to the story told to Mr and Mrs Hall about Burrishoole Abbey.

Murrisk Abbey

Murrisk Abbey was allegedly founded in 1456 by the Augustinian friars because 'the inhabitants of those parts have not hitherto been instructed in the faith'. The land was granted to the friars by Hugh O'Malley. Soon after its foundation it probably became popular to begin the pilgrimage to Croagh Patrick at Murrisk. The land was granted to the Garveys in 1578, some years after the Dissolution of the Monasteries, but the friars may have been allowed to stay

Pl. 104—Murrisk Abbey, holy water stoup.

throughout this period. Two chalices were presented to the friars at the abbey in the seventeenth century. One was the Viscount Mayo Chalice of 1635; the other was commissioned in 1648 by John de Burgo, an Augustinian friar, and made in Galway. The ruins of the abbey have changed little since it was visited by Gabriel Beranger and Angelo Maria Bigari in 1779. Their original paintings do not survive; however, in Grose's *Antiquities of Ireland* (1796) is an engraved drawing of Burrishoole Abbey copied in 1793 from an original painting by Bigari.

The ruins consist of an L-shaped building representing the church, the sacristy and the chapter room with overhead dormitory. The church is long and narrow, a shape typical of Augustinian churches. There is no sign of an internal division between nave and chancel, but there may originally have been a timber rood screen, of which no trace survives today. There is a beautiful east window, with carved human heads on the wall outside. In the south wall, which is crowned with unusual battlements, are a number of fine trefoil-headed and ogee-headed windows with elaborate external hood-mouldings. Towards the west end of the south wall is a simple doorway into the church. At west end of the church was a belfry tower inserted after the completion of the church, which must have fallen sometime in antiquity and was outlived by the earlier church. The springing of a ribbed vault is all that survives of this tower. Such towers were normally situated at the division of the church between nave and chancel, towards the east end, rather than the western position here at Murrisk.

At the east end of the church is a small door in the north wall with a holy water stoup nearby. The door gives access to the sacristy and a stone stairs leading to the dormitory on the first floor. North of the sacristy is the chapter room, where friars met to discuss business and read daily the chapter of the order's rule. There are no traces of domestic buildings such as the refectory, kitchen or cellars. The L-shaped plan of the surviving building suggests that there had been (intended at least) a cloister north of the church, but no trace survives today.

Castles

Ballyknock

Today there is no trace of the MacPhilbin castle of Ballyknock, sometimes called Bawn Castle, on the shores of Clew Bay, near Carraholly. The castle seems to have been already in ruins by the time of the Stafford Inquisition of 1635. The sources also mention a nearby settlement called Brae or Bruyh and an area called Cregganegolloglagh, derived from the Irish *Cregean na golloglagh*, meaning the 'rocky land of the gallowglasses'. This land may have been reserved for the mercenary soldiers (gallowglasses) hired by the MacGibbons, who owned Ballyknock Castle in the sixteenth century. It was at Ballyknock Castle in February 1580 that Grace O'Malley entered negotiations with Sir Nicholas Malby, the English governor of Connacht. Malby had come to the region with a large army in order to quash a rebellion by the Burkes.

Brockagh

All that survives of Brockagh Castle near Fahy is the south-west corner of a building, probably a tower-house built by the MacGibbons in the fifteenth or sixteenth century. The masonry stands 4m high, and there is a slight batter externally. The only feature remaining is an embrasure for a window that has been robbed out. There are impressions of plank-centring in the mortar of the soffit of the arch over the embrasure. The 1838 OS six-inch map shows the castle as a complete building, rectangular in plan. The castle overlooks the Owenabrokagh River, and in 1838 there were bleach, corn and tuck mills along this river. No doubt there were mills here in the medieval period also. In the Stafford Inquisition of 1635 it is called the 'ruinous castle of Ballygurrissy'.

Carrowmore

On top of a knoll in Carrowmore, south of Louisburgh, was the site of a castle known as *Caisleán Ghráinne*, probably because of a tradition that associated it with Grace O'Malley. This castle was sometimes called the Island of Carrowmore, and there was a small lake here in 1838 that has since been drained. Indeed, there was probably a more extensive lake here before this time, which is reflected in several local placenames, such as Callacuan, *caladh cuan*, meaning 'the marshy ground of the harbour'. The Stafford Inquisition (1635) states that there was 'a castle, island and watermill'. Only the foundation stones of parts of the castle remain, the walls having been pulled down and the stones used to build modern sheds.

Castleaffy

Castleaffy stands guard on an isolated inlet of Clew Bay with sheltered waters for harbouring ships. The castle was probably built by the MacTibbots at the end of the fifteenth century and was described in the Stafford Inquisition of 1635 as consisting of a 'castle, bawne and barbican'. Only half of the castle, a tower-house, survives relatively intact, the other half having collapsed. Local tradition tells that this was caused by enemy cannon fire, and the cannonballs have allegedly been found nearby. However, the castle seems to have been complete in 1838, when the Ordnance Survey mapped the area. The entrance to the castle was through a pointed-arched doorway on the west side. Above the door, in the ceiling of the entrance passage, is a murder-hole. On the right a stairwell extended upwards within the thickness of the walls, but the steps have been robbed out. This stairs gave access to the first-floor level. On the first floor is a short passage in the thickness of the east wall, giving access to a garderobe. The passage is lit by two narrow window loops, one of which has a slop tray. The first floor is spanned by a fine barrel vault, which forms the floor of the second storey. Outside the doorway to the castle is a raised platform. It seems that this platform represents the site of the bawn and barbican mentioned in the Stafford Inquisition.

Clare Island

Overlooking the sheltered harbour at Clare Island is a fine example of a tower-house built by the O'Malleys in the sixteenth century. During the medieval period the O'Malley ships probably landed on the sandy beach nearby. There is a legend that the tower was struck by lightning in 1750, killing a dog at the feet of the O'Malley who owned the castle and as a result abandoned the site. The castle was converted in around 1826 to a police barrack. The restoration is evidenced by the purple slate flashing on the two bartizans projecting from opposite angles of the tower. None of the original windows or fireplaces survives, and the main entrance is a later modification. To the left of the main entrance is a mural passage with stone stairs beginning at first-floor level. Access to the stone stairs may have been via a wooden staircase from the ground floor. At first-floor level is the main living room, and from here access could be gained to the bartizans and a garderobe. In the collections of the National Library of Ireland is a very early photograph of the castle taken by Edward Tenison in around 1858. The photograph shows the castle with its reconstructed roof and chimneys of 1826.

Corraunboy

In the grounds of Burrishoole House, looking across the small bay to Burrishoole Abbey, are the remains of a castle known as Tyremore in the thirteenth century. The castle was built by the Butlers, probably soon after their arrival here in 1235. In the thirteenth century it was attacked and burned by the O'Conors. The Butlers remained there until around 1333, when they finally abandoned the castle, although they retained ownership of the land until the seventeenth century. *The Compossicion Booke of Conought* (1585) indicates that the castle had the status of a manor in the sixteenth century. In a grant to Thomas, earl of Ormond, by James I in 1612 the manor of Burrishoole was described as containing one ruinous 'fortress or castle' and a bawn. However, an earlier inquisition, of 1333, suggests that Burrishoole was a cantred of the manor of Loughrea, Co. Galway, and not originally an independent manor.

The castle remains consist of a large lump of masonry, rubble built, 8m long and *c.* 6m high. The outer face of the wall has been robbed out, and no architectural features survive; however, at the north-east extremity of the wall is a smooth face with the remains of the springing of an arch. This may be the remains of an embrasure for a window loop or a doorway.

In 1838 John O'Donovan of the Ordnance Survey was told that the Butler castle was situated in Carrowkeel, north of Burrishoole Abbey, but it is more likely that the remains at Burrishoole House are those of the Butler castle. The castle was abandoned by the Butlers sometime after 1333 and may have remained uninhabited after this period. It was probably a ruin by 1580, when Malby chose to fortify the abbey instead.

Doon

Doon Castle may be the castle mentioned in the Annals of Connaught and the Annals of the Four Masters as Dún Mugdord, where the Anglo-Normans set up a garrison and from here confronted Manus O'Conor in 1235. The identification with Doon Castle is not clear, but if it is correct it suggests that the castle was built on an earlier fortification of some kind. All that survives are two lumps of masonry at the edge of a crescent-shaped area on top of the hill. Unfortunately, there is no evidence of the date of the building, and its original plan is not certain. There are strong traditions of there having been a cave at this site that has been blocked up, which may be the remains of a souterrain, perhaps associated with an earlier ringfort at the site.

Rockfleet

The Burke tower house at Rockfleet Bay is one of the most picturesque castles in the country, and the roof and wooden floors have been carefully reconstructed. The sixteenth-century castle was the home of Grace O'Malley at various times following her marriage to Richard Burke at the end of the sixteenth century. The nearby sheltered bay provided ideal anchorage for the O'Malley fleet. There are many traditions that tell of a hole through the wall on the top floor where a cable passed to moor a vessel to Grace's bed, that she might be instantly alerted in the event of trouble. In 1579 Granuaile successfully repulsed an attack on the castle by a garrison from Galway led by Captain Martin. Interestingly, a field nearby in Gortfahy is still known as *an parc dhearg*, meaning 'the red field', and is traditionally regarded as the site of a battle.

Entrance to the tower is via a small, simple, Gothic-arched door, and access to the first floor is via a wooden ladder. The top of the ladder is defended by a gun-loop behind the head. This gun-loop is reached by a narrow passage within the thickness of the wall. The main first-floor room has three windows with large embrasures. In the soffits of the embrasures are the impressions in the mortar of the wickerwork frame used in their construction. Access from the first floor to the tower is via a stone spiral staircase, which leads to a good

*Pl. 105—Rockfleet
tower-house.*

example of a garderobe and two mural passages providing flanking defences of
the landward side of the castle. There is also a large storage room roofed with
a fine barrel vault, with excellently preserved impressions in the mortar of the
wickerwork frame used to construct the vault. The top floor has a fine fireplace
and a door that could be used instead of the narrow staircase to haul up goods
or cargoes brought in by the ships below. From here access could be gained to
the battlements, which are defended by two machicolations overhanging the
walls.

Today all that remains is the tower, but originally there was a bawn wall and perhaps a barbican. These features survived in 1842, when Mr and Mrs Samuel Carter Hall visited the castle and claimed that 'the whole character of the building [is] that of savage strength. It stands upon the rock, and appears to have been protected by a strong surrounding wall, a small circular tower adjoining it being built in the remains of this wall.' Several corbels project from the outside of the north-western side of the tower and seem to indicate that a low building was attached here, perhaps a hall for entertaining guests.

Toberrooaun

On top of a knoll in Toberrooaun townland are the ruins of a castle known as MacPhilbins' Castle, and sometimes called Aille Castle in the old documents (Aille is now the name of a neighbouring townland). The ruins consist of the remains of an ivy-covered tower, perhaps a late fifteenth-century or early sixteenth-century tower-house. There is no clear dating evidence for the construction of this tower, which is in the north-west angle of a later bawn. The bawn wall survives quite well preserved along the east and south-east. At the top of this wall along the north-east are the remains of steps (robbed out) that gave access to a walkway along the top of the wall, which is crowned with broken-down battlements. At the south end of this wall is a large hole where the

Pl. 106—MacPhilbins' castle, Toberrooaun.

entrance was, but all the cut stones have been robbed out. Only the remains of draw-bar holes on either side survive. In the south-east angle of this bawn wall is a gun-loop, suggesting a date in the sixteenth century for its construction.

Glossary

AUMBRY: A small cupboard or *niche* used for storing vessels needed for the conduct of Mass.

BARBICAN: A forework for defending the gateway to a castle.

BARTIZAN: A roofed, floorless turret projecting from the corner of a castle, either at roof level or below, to defend the angles and provide flanking fire.

BATTER: Receding upward slope of the outer face of a wall.

BATTLEMENTS: A *parapet*, usually divided into short, solid merlons by regular openings or embrasures. Also called crenellation.

BAWN: Walled enclosure around a castle or tower-house, forming a defended yard.

BOSS: Small domed projection.

BULLAUN: Hollowed-out basin in the surface of a stone, usually an unshaped boulder.

BUTTRESS: A mass of masonry projecting from or built against a wall to give additional strength.

CAPSTONE: A large stone or slab covering a megalithic tomb.

CHANCEL: The eastern portion of a church, where the altar is situated. Often a separate compartment within the body of a church. The chancel arch is that which separates the *nave* from the chancel.

CHEVRON: A V-shaped ornament, producing a zigzag effect in succession.

CHI-RHO: Monogram of Christ's name in Greek characters.

CLOCHAUN: A small stone building, rounded in plan with the roof corbelled inwards in successive courses like a beehive.

CORBEL: Stone projecting from a wall, which supports floor beams, rafters or oversailing masonry.

DRESSED: Roughly faced and shaped stone.

DRYSTONE: Coursed or uncoursed masonry constructed without mortar.

EMBRASURE: Recess for a doorway or window, or an opening in a parapet wall.

FALSE RELIEF: Sculpture whereby carvings appear to be in relief although they are actually no higher than the general surface.

GALLERY (megalithic tomb): An oblong or wedge-shaped compartment in which burials were deposited.

GARDEROBE: Medieval lavatory.

HOOD-MOULDING: The projecting moulding placed around the top of a window, door or arch.

JAMB: The side of an arch, doorway or window.

KEEP: The principal tower of a castle.

KERB: Continuous line of stones or slabs surrounding the base of a cairn.

LINTEL: A horizontal stone covering a doorway.

LOOP: A small narrow light, of various forms, in a wall or at the angle of two walls, facilitating the release of projectiles such as arrows or gunshot.

MACHICOLATION: A projecting *parapet* supported on *corbels* between which stones etc. could be dropped on assailants.

MORTISE: A hole made to receive and secure the end of another part, such as a *tenon*.

MULLION: The vertical post that divides a window into two or more lights.

MURDER-HOLE: An aperture in the ceiling above the main entrance to a castle through which intruders could be fired upon.

NAVE: The main, western portion of a church, often a separate compartment from the *chancel*.

NICHE: A recess in a wall.

OGEE-HEADED: Arch over a window formed with reversed curves, giving an onion-shaped head.

OGHAM: An ancient Irish alphabet.

ORTHOSTAT: Upright block of stone used to form the sides of chambers or passages in megalithic tombs.

PALISADE: A fence of timber stakes.

PARAPET: A low wall placed at the edge of a roof for protection, sometimes crenellated.

PISCINA: A basin in a church with a drainhole for washing the sacred vessels.

PUTLOG HOLE: An opening left in a wall for the insertion of scaffolding.

SEPTAL STONE: A large large slab separating the portico from the main chamber in a wedge tomb.

SHERDS: Fragments of pottery.

SOFFIT: The underside of an arch or lintel.

SPLAY: Sides of a window opening with obtuse or acute angles to the other wall faces.

SPRINGING: The starting point of the curve of an arch or vault.

STOUP: A vessel to contain holy water, near a church doorway.

TENON: A projecting piece of stone or wood, fitting into a socket or *mortise*.

TRACERY: The ornamental intersecting work of stone in the upper part of a window.

TREFOIL: A three-lobed arch or a three-leafed motif.

VAULT: An arched structure of masonry usually forming a ceiling or roof.

WALL-WALK: A walkway positioned outside the roof and behind the *parapet* of a castle or church.

WICKER-CENTRING: A temporary wicker framework used to support an arch or vault while it is under construction.

Bibliography

Armstrong, E.C.R. 1917 Bronze seal matrix found in Burrishoole Friary. *Journal of the Royal Society of Antiquaries of Ireland* **47**, 185–6.

Ballintubber Abbey 1989 *Tóchar Phádraig. Patrick's Causeway from Ballintubber to Croagh Patrick, a pilgrim's progress.* Ballintubber Abbey Publications.

Barrow, G.L. 1979 *The round towers of Ireland.* Academy Press, Dublin.

Barrow, J. 1836 *A tour round Ireland, through the sea-coast counties, in the autumn of 1835.* London.

Bartlett, W.H. n.d. *The scenery and antiquities of Ireland.* James S. Virtue, London.

Blake, M.J. 1928 Some old silver chalices connected with the counties of Galway and Mayo. *Journal of the Royal Society of Antiquaries of Ireland* **58**, 22–43.

Bourke, E. 1995 *Burke, Bourke & de Burgh: people and places* (3rd edn). Ballinakella Press, Whitegate, and De Burca Rare Books, Blackrock.

Bracken, G.G. and Wayman, P.A. 1992 A Neolithic or Bronze-Age alignment for Croagh Patrick. *Cathair na Mart* **12**, 1–12.

Buckley, J.J. 1939 Some Irish altar plate. *Journal of the Royal Society of Antiquaries of Ireland* **69**, supplement, 1–80.

Cahill, M. 1988 A preliminary account of a Later Bronze Age hoard from Kilbride, Co. Mayo. *Cathair na Mart* **8**, 26–9.

Chambers, A. 1998 *Granuaile: the life and times of Grace O'Malley c. 1530–1603.* Wolfhound Press, Dublin.

Corlett, C. 1993 Previously unrecorded cross-slab from Feenune in the barony of Murrisk, County Mayo. *Journal of the Royal Society of Antiquaries of Ireland* **123**, 169–70.

Corlett, C. 1996 Prehistoric pilgrimage to Croagh Patrick. *Cathair na Mart* **16**, 54–61.

Corlett, C. 1997a Prehistoric pilgrimage to Croagh Patrick. *Archaeology Ireland* **11** (2), 8–11.

Corlett, C. 1997b The prehistory of the parish of Kilgeever, south-west County Mayo. *Journal of the Galway Archaeological and Historical Society* **49**, 65–103.

Corlett, C. 1997c An Early Christian ecclesiastical site at Carrowrevagh, near Carrowkennedy, County Mayo. *Cathair na Mart* **17**, 115–20.

Corlett, C. 1998 A survey of the standing stone complex at Killadangan, County Mayo. *Journal of the Galway Archaeological and Historical Society* **50**, 135–50.

Coxon, P. and O'Connell, M. (eds) 1994 *Clare Island and Inishbofin.* Irish Association for Quaternary Studies, Dublin.

Curtis, E. 1934 Seventeenth century documents relating of the manors of Aughrim and Burrishoole. *Journal of the Galway Archaeological and Historical Society* **16**, 48–56.

D'Alton, Revd 1928 *The history of the archdiocese of Tuam.* Dublin.

De Valera, R. and Ó Nualláin, S. 1964 *Survey of the megalithic tombs of Ireland, vol. II. Co. Mayo.* Stationery Office, Dublin.

Duffy, F. 1999 Westport estate and town: an example of planned settlement according to picturesque principles: part 1. *Cathair na Mart* **19**, 48–64.

Egan, J. (ed.) 1997 *Killeen church and people.* Killeen Community Council.

Ellis, H. 1838 'A description of the province of Connaught', dated in the month of 'January, 1612' from a volume of the Lansdowne Manuscripts, preserved in the British Museum, No. 255. *Archaeologia* **27**, 124–34.

Eogan, G. 1965 *Catalogue of Irish bronze swords.* The Stationery Office, Dublin.

Eogan, G. 1983 *Hoards of the Irish Later Bronze Age.* University College Dublin.

Eogan, G. 1994 *The accomplished art.* Oxbow Monograph 42. Oxbow Books, Oxford.

Falvey, A. 1999 Mayo workhouses and lunatic asylums. *Cathair na Mart* **19**, 65–76.

Freeman, A.M. (ed.) 1936 *The Compossicion Booke of Conought.* The Stationery Office, Dublin.

Freeman, A.M. (ed.) 1970 *The annals of Connaught (AD 1224–1544).* Dublin Institute for Advanced Studies.

Gibbons, M. and Higgins, J. 1991 Some observations on the Sites and Monuments Record of County Mayo. *Cathair na Mart* **11**, 1–20.

Gibbons, M. and Higgins, J. 1993 Three western Islands. *Archaeology Ireland* **7** (2), 20–3.

Gosling, P. 1990 The archaeology of Clare Island, Co. Mayo. *Archaeology Ireland* **4** (1), 7–12.

Gosling, P. (ed.) 1993 *New Survey of Clare Island 1991–1995, Archaeological Section.* Royal Irish Academy, Dublin.

Grose, F. 1796 *The antiquities of Ireland.* M. Hooper, London.

Hall, Mr and Mrs S.C. 1843 *Ireland: its scenery, character, &c* (3 vols). London.

Hall, R. 1973 A hoard of Viking silver bracelets from Cushalogurt, Co. Mayo. *Journal of the Royal Society of Antiquaries of Ireland* **103**, 78–85.

Hamrock, I. (ed.) 1998 *The Famine in Mayo, 1845–1850.* Mayo County Council, Castlebar.

Harbison, P. 1991 *Pilgrimage in Ireland, the monuments and the people.* Barrie and Jenkins, London.

Hennessy, W.M. (ed.) 1871 *The annals of Loch Cé: a chronicle of Irish affairs from A.D. 1014 to A.D. 1590* (2 vols). London.

Hennessy, W.M. and MacCarthy, B. (ed.) 1887–1901 *Annals of Ulster* (4 vols). Dublin.

Henry, F. 1937 Early Christian slabs and pillar stones in the west of Ireland. *Journal of the Royal Society of Antiquaries of Ireland* **57**, 265–79.

Henry, F. 1947 The antiquities of Caher Island (Co. Mayo). *Journal of the Royal Society of Antiquaries of Ireland* **77**, 23–38.

Henry, F. 1952 Megalithic and Early Christian remains at Lankill, Co. Mayo. *Journal of the Royal Society of Antiquaries of Ireland* **82**, 68–71.

Herity, M. 1974 *Irish passage graves.* Irish University Press, Dublin.

Herity, M. 1989 Cathair na Naomh and its cross-slabs. *Cathair na Mart* **9**, 91–100.

Herity, M. 1995a Two island hermitages in the Atlantic: Rathlin O'Birne, Donegal, and Caher Island, Mayo. *Journal of the Royal Society of Antiquaries of Ireland* **125**, 85–128.

Herity, M. 1995b The chi-rho and other early cross-forms in Ireland. In J.-M. Picard (ed.), *Aquitaine and Ireland in the Middle Ages*, 233–60. Four Courts Press, Dublin.

Higgins, J. 1995 A miniature Early Christian stone cross from Kilgeever, Co. Mayo. *Cathair na Mart* **15**, 70–6.

Higgins, J. and Gibbons, M. 1993 Early Christian monuments at Kilgeever, Co. Mayo. *Cathair na Mart* **13**, 32–44.

Horgan, G.M. (ed.) 1988 *Tales of the west of Ireland, by James Berry*. Colin Smyth, Buckinghamshire.

Hughes, H. 1991 *Croagh Patrick (Cruach Phádraig—The Reek): an ancient mountain pilgrimage*. Harry Hughes, Westport.

Hutton, A.W. (ed.) 1970 *Arthur Young: a tour in Ireland 1776–1779*. Irish University Press, Shannon.

Irwin, M. 1998 An early medieval church site at Kilbree Upper, Sheeaune, Westport, Co. Mayo. *Cathair na Mart* **18**, 44–8.

Jordan, A.J. 1991 *Major John MacBride, 1865–1916*. Westport Historical Society.

Jordan, D.E. 1994 *Land and popular politics in Ireland. County Mayo from the Plantation to the Land War*. Cambridge University Press.

Joyce, B. 1999 Early ecclesiastical site at Farburren, parish of Oughaval, Co. Mayo. *Cathair na Mart* **19**, 86–97.

Kelly, J. 1995 *'That damn'd thing called honour': duelling in Ireland 1570–1860*. Cork University Press.

Kelly, W.E. 1897 Inscribed pillar-stones, County Mayo. *Journal of the Royal Society of Antiquaries of Ireland* **27**, 185–7.

Kinahan, G.H. 1870–9 New (?) type of clochaun, and a remarkable cross, south-ward of Louisburg, Co. Mayo. *Proceedings of the Royal Irish Academy* **15**, 69.

Knox, H.T. 1899 Tobernahaltora, near Louisburg. *Journal of the Royal Society of Antiquaries of Ireland* **29**, 63–4.

Knox, H.T. 1904a *Notes on the early history of the dioceses of Tuam, Killala and Achonry*. Hodges Figgis, Dublin.

Knox, H.T. 1904b Carved stone in Knappaghmanagh, County Mayo. *Journal of the Royal Society of Antiquaries of Ireland* **34**, 70–1.

Knox, H.T. 1908 *The history of the county of Mayo to the close of the sixteenth century*. Hodges Figgis, Dublin.

Knox, H.T. 1919 St. Marcan's loch and ruins. *Journal of the Royal Society of Antiquaries of Ireland* **49**, 89–91.

Lalor, B. 1999 *The Irish round tower: origins and architecture explored*. Collins Press, Cork.

Lawless, C. 1990 A *fulacht fiadh*? Bronze Age cooking experiment at Turlough, Castlebar. *Cathair na Mart* **10**, 1–10.

Leask, H.G. 1943 Murrisk Abbey, Co. Mayo. *Journal of the Royal Society of Antiquaries of Ireland* **73**, 137–41.

Lyons, J. 1995 *Louisburgh: a history.* Louisburgh Traders Association.

McCabe, D. 1995 Westport. In A. Simms and J.H. Andrews (eds), *More Irish country towns*, 132–4. Mercier Press, Dublin.

Mac Cárthaigh, C. and Whelan, K. (eds) 1999 *New survey of Clare Island, vol. 1. History and cultural landscape.* Royal Irish Academy, Dublin.

McNally, J. 1998 *Westport: the tear & the smile.* Berry Print Group, Westport.

MacNeill, M. 1962 *The festival of Lughnasa: a study of the survival of the Celtic festival of the beginning of the harvest.* Oxford University Press, London.

MacParlan, J. 1802 *Statistical survey of Mayo drawn up in 1801.* The Dublin Society.

McVeigh, J. (ed.) 1995 *Richard Pococke's Irish tours.* Irish Academic Press, Dublin.

Mannion, B. 1988 Aughagower and its patrician sites and connections. *Cathair na Mart* **8**, 5–18.

Mayock, J. 1998 William Leeson: Westport's first town planner. *Cathair na Mart* **18**, 135–42.

Morahan, L. 1998 A wealth of monuments from the Croagh Patrick archaeological survey. *Cathair na Mart* **18**, 143–50.

Mulloy, S. 1988 *O'Malley people and places.* Ballinakella Press, Whitegate, and Carrowbaun Press, Westport.

Mulloy, S. 1999 *Father Manus Sweeney: a Mayo priest in the rebellion of 1798.* Westport Historical Society.

Murphy, S. 1986 The Sligo Papers, Westport House, Co. Mayo. *Analecta Hibernica* **33**, 15–46.

Nicholson, A. 1851 *Lights and shades of Ireland: annals of the Famine of 1847, 1848 and 1849.* New York.

O'Donovan, J. (ed.) 1851 *Annála Ríoghachta Éireann. Annals of the kingdom of Ireland by the Four Masters from the earliest period to the year 1616* (7 vols). Dublin.

O'Flanagan, M. 1926 Letters relating to the antiquities of the county of Mayo containing information collected during the progress of the Ordnance Survey in 1838, vol. 1. Unpublished typescript.

O'Hara, B. (ed.) 1982 *Mayo: aspects of its heritage.* Galway.

Ó Muraíle, N. 1985 *Mayo places: their name and origins.* Westport.

Ó Nualláin, S. 1972 A Neolithic house at Ballyglass, near Ballycastle, Co. Mayo. *Journal of the Royal Society of Antiquaries of Ireland* **102**, 49–57.

Ó Ríordáin, S.P. and Mac Dermott, M. 1950–1 The excavation of a ring-fort at Letterkeen, Co. Mayo. *Proceedings of the Royal Irish Academy* **54**C, 89–119.

O'Sullivan, W. 1958 *The Stafford Inquisition of County Mayo.* Dublin.

Otway, C. 1839 *A tour of Connaught.* William Curry Junior, Dublin.

Quinn, J.F. 1993 *History of Mayo, vol. 2.* Brendan Quinn, Ballina.

Rhys, Principal 1898 Some ogam-stones in Connaught. *Journal of the Royal Society of Antiquaries of Ireland* **28**, 230–6.

Rolleston, T.W. 1900 The church of St Patrick on Caher Island, County Mayo. *Journal of the Royal Society of Antiquaries of Ireland* **30**, 357–63.

Russell, T.O. 1897 *Beauties and antiquities of Ireland.* London.

Rynne, E. 1954–6 'Turnincorragh': a Bronze Age burial mound in Co. Mayo. *Journal of the Galway Archaeological and Historical Society* **26**, 72–4.

Simington, R.C. 1956 *Books of Survey and Distribution, 1636–1703, vol. II. County of Mayo.* Irish Manuscripts Commission, Dublin.

Stevenson, J. (ed.) 1917 *A Frenchman's walk through Ireland 1796–7.* Dublin.

Thackeray, W.M. 1843 *The Irish sketch-book.* London.

Van Hoek, M.A.M. 1993 The prehistoric rock art of the Boheh Stone, Co. Mayo. *Cathair na Mart* **13**, 1–15.

Van Hoek, M.A.M. 1995 The keyhole-pattern in the prehistoric rock art of Ireland and Britain. *Cathair na Mart* **15**, 15–25.

Walsh, G. 1994 Preliminary report on the archaeological excavations on the summit of Croagh Patrick, 1994. *Cathair na Mart* **14**, 1–10.

Walsh, G. 1996 'Croagh Patrick, Glaspatrick/Teevenacroagh'. In I. Bennet (ed.), *Excavations 1995*, 67–8. Wordwell, Bray.

Westropp, T.J. 1911 Clare Island Survey 2: history and archaeology. *Proceedings of the Royal Irish Academy* **31**, 1–78.

Wilde, W.R. 1870–71 Memoir of Gabriel Beranger, and his labours in the cause of Irish art, literature, and antiquities from 1760 to 1780, with illustrations. *Journal of the Royal Society of Antiquaries of Ireland* **11**, 121–52.

Index